ENTERPRISE

02.08

The
Entrepreneurial
Individual

Roger Cartwright

- *The* fast track route to acquiring the skills and tactics of the world's most successful entrepreneurs

- Covers all the critical entrepreneurial attributes, from vision to commitment, and from risk taking to customer focus

- Examples and lessons from some of the world's most successful entrepreneurs, including Richard Branson, Ken Bogas and Kwek Leng Beng, and ideas from the smartest thinkers, including Stephen Covey, Peter Drucker and Tom Peters

- Includes a glossary of key concepts and a comprehensive resources guide

essential management thinking at your fingertips

The right of Roger Cartwright to be identified as the author of this work has been asserted in accordance with the Copyright, Designs and Patents Act 1988

First published 2002 by
Capstone Publishing (A Wiley Company)
8 Newtec Place
Magdalen Road
Oxford OX4 1RE
United Kingdom
http://www.capstoneideas.com

CIP catalogue records for this book are available from the British Library and the US Library of Congress

ISBN 1-84112-245-9

This book is printed on acid-free paper

Substantial discounts on bulk quantities of Capstone books are available to corporations, professional associations and other organizations. Please contact Capstone for more details on +44 (0)1865 798 623 or (fax) +44 (0)1865 240 941 or (e-mail) info@wiley-capstone.co.uk

Contents

Contents

Introduction to ExpressExec

ExpressExec is 3 million words of the latest management thinking compiled into 10 modules. Each module contains 10 individual titles forming a comprehensive resource of current business practice written by leading practitioners in their field. From brand management to balanced scorecard, ExpressExec enables you to grasp the key concepts behind each subject and implement the theory immediately. Each of the 100 titles is available in print and electronic formats.

Through the ExpressExec.com Website you will discover that you can access the complete resource in a number of ways:

» printed books or e-books;
» e-content – PDF or XML (for licensed syndication) adding value to an intranet or Internet site;
» a corporate e-learning/knowledge management solution providing a cost-effective platform for developing skills and sharing knowledge within an organization;
» bespoke delivery – tailored solutions to solve your need.

Why not visit www.expressexec.com and register for free key management briefings, a monthly newsletter and interactive skills checklists. Share your ideas about ExpressExec and your thoughts about business today.

Please contact elound@wiley-capstone.co.uk for more information.

Introduction to the Entrepreneurial Individual

» This material is about the entrepreneurial individual who may or may not work for an entrepreneurial organization.
» Entrepreneurship is concerned with growth.
» Growth nearly always involves risk.
» For every high profile entrepreneur there are many others working on a smaller scale.

An entrepreneur is a person who is prepared to take a calculated risk on a business venture in which they have a belief and, if the venture is a success, to plough the profits back into further ventures or, if it is a failure, to treat the experience as part of learning and continue to pursue their vision.

The entrepreneurial individual is often to be found at the forefront of innovation running their own organization; indeed this is where they are happiest as this is where the buzz is. There are those, however, who work either for other entrepreneurs or for more traditional organizations. The differences between traditional and entrepreneurial organizations are covered in companion material in *ExpressExec: Creating the Entrepreneurial Organization*.

Entrepreneurs are vital to business progress. George Bernard Shaw is reputed to have remarked that all progress is dependent upon unreasonable people. Reasonable people adapt their behavior to the world whilst the unreasonable persist in trying to adapt the world to themselves. Therefore, Shaw argued, progress and change depend upon the unreasonable. Entrepreneurs are unreasonable because they do not accept the status quo and conventional thinking but introduce new ideas both in terms of products and services and the way in which they are delivered. The entrepreneur and his or her organization seek out opportunities and act on them, taking a risk (normally carefully calculated and analyzed) where necessary. Failure is accepted as a natural consequence of the entrepreneurial culture and is something to learn from and turn to eventual profit. Taking risks is not an attribute common to all people; many try to minimize the risks they take in their working or even personal lives. Paradoxically, the entrepreneur as a risk-taker needs people around him or her who are less prone to risk-taking and who can cope with the tedious and mundane tasks that the entrepreneur may dislike but which need to be carried out in the normal course of business.

Whilst it is easy to recognize an entrepreneur such as Bill Gates of Microsoft and Sir Richard Branson, the founder of the Virgin Group in the UK, a group that includes the airline Virgin Atlantic, by their high profile, there are others who are less well-known but just as entrepreneurial and there are very many who have entrepreneurial tendencies. Entrepreneurship is not an either-or state but a continuum.

This material is designed to assist you in moving along the continuum towards the entrepreneurial end. In doing so you will need to examine your own behavior and personality and may need to take risks, small ones at first and then perhaps larger ones. The risks that entrepreneurs take may seem large but they are nearly always calculated. Branson himself states that the risk to the Virgin Group of operating his airline for one year using leased aircraft was only £2mn (about $3.2mn), i.e. less than a third of the 1984 profit. He deemed that this was an acceptable risk to take and has been proved correct. Taking risks, however, means making mistakes at some time but it is said that the person who never made a mistake never made anything!

What is the Entrepreneurial Individual?

» Entrepreneurship is more than just wealth creation; it is also about forward movement, innovation, and enjoyment.
» The motivation for an entrepreneur may well be more concerned with recognition and achievement.
» Entrepreneurs need attributes of vision, commitment, self-belief, discipline, risk-taking, concern for the customer, and creativity.
» Entrepreneurial skills center on analysis, networking, building relationships, negotiation, selling, and finance.
» The successful entrepreneur compensates for any lack of skills by acquiring the services and commitment of others who possess those skills. Those people are then valued.
» The entrepreneur who generates customer demand and then fails to deliver fully is going to fail.
» Entrepreneurs must communicate their vision to all those who work with them.

This material is about the attributes and skills required for entrepreneurship. Entrepreneurship can be defined as a business philosophy that is concerned with growth, is proactive rather than reactive, customer-focused, accepts the risks involved in a venture and then takes risks that seem likely to bring sustained growth and market share, is prepared to tolerate failure, and, lastly, has a large number of its employees who share the vision and believe in the same values and ideas as the entrepreneur himself or herself.

The attributes that will be considered in this material are those of:

» vision
» commitment
» self-belief
» discipline
» risk-taking
» concern for the customer
» creativity.

Whilst the skills center on:

» analysis
» networking
» building relationships
» negotiation
» selling
» finance.

It is well-known that skills can be learnt and developed but what of attributes? Are they innate or can they also be developed? It is fair to say that there are some who could never be an entrepreneur, and those for whom it is a natural state of affairs. However, in between are a large number of people, perhaps the majority, who have latent attributes that need bringing out and developing for them to become entrepreneurs, perhaps in a small way but entrepreneurs nevertheless.

Entrepreneurial activity is something that can start early in a working life, as with Gates and Branson who both began their entrepreneurial activities whilst still at high school, or can develop later on in life following a lay-off or even retirement. The UK entrepreneur Adam

Faith was once a successful rock star with a long singing career behind him and has now found a new niche in life – he has made a new name as an investment advisor. Walker founded Priceline when he was in his forties, Davis was thirty-nine when he joined Lycos. What characterizes entrepreneurs is a will to succeed and motivating factors that are (as will be shown in this material) more related to achievement and recognition than to pure monetary gain. William Heinecke (see Chapters 6 and 8) has noted that, serious as business is, for the entrepreneur it should also be fun. After all, they are doing what they enjoy!

One major way in which the entrepreneurial individual differs from others in the world of business and commerce is in the use of profits and the dynamics of the enterprise. For the entrepreneurial individual, forward motion towards a goal is all-important and, like any forward motion, that requires an input of fuel. At least in the early stages of their entrepreneurial career the entrepreneurial individual will plough much of the profits of the enterprise back into sustaining and even increasing the forward motion. Later these profits may be used to start up and subscribe to other ventures.

In a book published in 2000, Tom Bower attacked the public reputation of Sir Richard Branson, an entrepreneur widely regarded as the UK's favorite business person and who has been quoted as the role model most parents wish their children to emulate. In the context of this text, whether Bower is right or wrong about Branson is irrelevant (and may well be decided by the courts). However, talking about somebody else involved in the Branson story, Bower states that this person could never have emulated Branson as he lacked ruthless energy, egoism, skill, instinct, and a compelling performance – characteristics that Bower attached to Branson.

Ruthless energy tends to be something that develops with success. Skills and performance can certainly be developed so that over half of the attributes Bower applies to Branson can be worked upon by an individual. If egoism is considered as self-belief, this is something that grows with success and thus only instinct is left as a difficult skill to develop. However, even instinct can be honed or improved so that with practice everybody can improve their entrepreneurial behavior if that is what they wish.

Various authorities have differing views of precisely what an entrepreneur is and what entrepreneurship involves.

» Mark Peterson, whilst not actually defining an entrepreneur in his book, *The Complete Entrepreneur* (1996), appears to see entrepreneurship mainly in terms of wealth creation.
» William Heinecke, in *The Entrepreneur* (2000), defines an entrepreneur as "... a person who gauges the risks and rewards of a business and works quickly to initiate and manage a particular opportunity, idea, or concept. The key words are risk and business. The entrepreneur will risk more, work harder and demand more of himself or herself than any ordinary business person. The rewards, however, can be immeasurable."
» Peter Drucker, in *Innovation and Entrepreneurship* (1985), puts considerable stress on the concept that "entrepreneurs innovate. Innovation is the specific instrument of entrepreneurship. It is the act that endows resources with a new capacity to create wealth." This fits in neatly with Sir Richard Branson's philosophy of finding a market that is not providing the best for its customers and then servicing that market in a different, more exciting, customer-centered way.
» Larry Farrell, in the 2001 edition of *The Entrepreneurial Age*, agrees with Drucker. Farrell states: "high-speed innovation is the entrepreneur's ultimate weapon..."

Innovation is not necessarily doing something new. It can be a new way of doing something old (or an old way of doing something new – using an older method to deliver a brand new product for instance). Part of the equation, however, needs to be the newness. If that newness corresponds to the needs and wants of the customer then the person delivering it to the customer is likely to reap all of the initial rewards – that person is an entrepreneur.

At the beginning of this chapter a series of entrepreneurial attributes and skills were introduced and indeed will be expanded in Chapter 6. Not everybody can develop expertise in all the skill areas and it is important for the entrepreneur to recognize his or her own weaknesses and to compensate for them by buying-in expertise and experience where necessary.

SPEED AND PEOPLE

High-speed innovation may not allow the entrepreneur to develop all the skills they need. In time these skills will develop. However, it may well be necessary for financial, marketing, administrative skills, etc., to be in place early on in a project. If customers are to be delighted and satisfied, all of the organizational processes must be in place before the product is offered to the public or else disappointment and disillusionment with the entrepreneur's performance can occur. The UK inventor and potential entrepreneur Sir Clive Sinclair developed the Spectrum microcomputer in the early 1980s. Potentially this was a major development but demand far exceeded supply and the organization was not capable of stepping up the rate of supply to retail outlets. Disappointment for customers and bad publicity for Sinclair and his organization resulted.

In order to avoid this type of problem, the relationship skills of the entrepreneur are all-important. If they do not possess any of the skills required to market or deliver their product or service they need to acquire the services and loyalty of people with those skills. Such people become more than mere employees. The entrepreneur must imbue them with their vision, as they are critical partners in the process. Companion material in the *ExpressExec* series, *Creating the Entrepreneurial Organization*, also stresses the importance of staff involved in routine processes. Whilst ordering supplies and paying salaries, etc., may not have the glamour of the more entrepreneurial aspects of the business, they are just as important. These may well be areas where the entrepreneur is deficient in skills. The answer is to buy-in the best people possible and remember that their contribution is as valuable as anybody else's.

The successful entrepreneur never forgets that their success is not just due to products, services, ideas, and concepts, but to the hard work of those working with them.

THE BUTTERFLY MIND

Tom Bower, quoted earlier, refers to Sir Richard Branson's "butterfly mind." This is not an uncommon epithet to apply to entrepreneurs. One has to consider what it is that provides entrepreneurs with the buzz and motivation to take business risks – what is their inspiration? The writer of this material would disagree with Peterson's assertion that it is the pursuit of wealth. There is more to the motivation of an entrepreneur than pure money. What do the Bill Gateses and Richard Bransons of this world really want? Bower does state that he believes that Branson wants to be loved and he may not be far wrong. The US industrial psychologist Frederick Herzberg believes that for managers at least the main motivators are achievement and recognition. His 1960 treatise, *Work and the Nature of Man*, suggested that money was not actually a motivator – it was a lack of sufficient remuneration that acted as a *de-motivator*. Once people had sufficient money to meet their needs and wants, other factors came into play, of which a recognition by peers and society and the thrill of achieving set goals were amongst the most important.

KEY LEARNING POINTS

» The key to understanding entrepreneurs lies in the importance of recognition and achievement as motivational factors.

» All staff, however mundane their role, are important in the entrepreneurial process.

» Entrepreneurs must consistently satisfy and delight their customers.

» Whilst entrepreneurship is rightly a business activity, many of its roots are psychological.

» Entrepreneurship is about moving forward and innovation.

The Evolution of Individual Entrepreneurship

» Entrepreneurism has been around since humans began trading with each other.

» Each period of history produces new opportunities for entrepreneurs.

» The great period of US entrepreneurship began after the Civil War and is still with us today.

» Entrepreneurs are not necessarily the inventors, discoverers, and explorers, but they serve a vital facilitating role.

There have been entrepreneurial individuals since the day when one human tribe first traded with another.

Throughout the history of business and commerce there have been those individuals who have seen opportunities and have grasped them, leading the way not only in terms of products and services but also in the ways in which those products and services have been delivered and the geographic and demographic areas of operation.

The *Parable of the Talents* in the Bible (Matthew 25:14–30) is actually an example of entrepreneurship. The good and faithful servant used what he had been given to make more. This is what entrepreneurship is about.

The entrepreneur is a tomorrow person in that they use part of the profits of today to feed into future developments, taking only what they need. Without the resources to fund developments there would be little progress in any field and thus we all owe a great debt to successive generations of entrepreneurs for many of the products and services we take for granted today.

EARLY ENTREPRENEURS

Much early entrepreneurship was in the field of trade. As groups and then nations began to explore the planet Earth they began to come into contact with other groups of humans. Whilst there was some fighting and taking of territory there was also the development of monetary and exchange systems to facilitate trade.

If a small community was self-sufficient in food, clothing, etc., then there was little need for trade but unfortunately the world's resources are not distributed equally. As the use of metals grew the possibility for trade also increased. Not every community would have ready access to the necessary ores and, whilst conquest might offer a solution to some, exchange and trade became more and more the means by which resources were acquired.

As communities grew from small settlements into towns, humankind also began to appreciate more and more luxury items. Clothing was not only for warmth, it could also provide useful visual signals about status – the imperial purple of ancient Rome is a good example – and a trade in cloths and silks developed.

Early human society soon began to differentiate membership into different occupational groups. There were rulers, merchants, artisans, scholars, traders, and a host of others. By medieval times these groups were clearly defined. The guilds that sprang up all over Europe in the twelfth to fourteenth centuries, each containing members of a particular profession and dedicated to supporting the members of that profession, were a very sophisticated means of both protecting the members and ensuring that high standards of workmanship were delivered to customers. The guilds were in effect both early unions and early watchdogs/regulators. They also presented great opportunities for those with an entrepreneurial approach to business.

Entrepreneurs were not (and are still not) necessarily inventors. Many inventors may be technologically brilliant and yet have little commercial acumen. The skill of the entrepreneur is in matching the creativity of the originator of a product, service, or development with the resources required to produce and deliver it to a customer, as shown in Fig. 3.1.

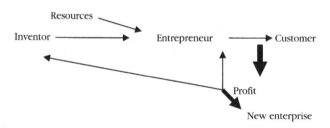

Fig. 3.1 The role of the entrepreneur.

The entrepreneurial role is essentially that of a middle man or woman but, unlike the wholesaler in the sales chain, the entrepreneurial individual will be constantly looking to employ profits in new enterprises.

ENTREPRENEURSHIP AND THE FINANCE FUNCTION

As commerce developed so there was a need for financial systems that could use credit and loans to support cash flow and finance ventures.

The difference between an entrepreneur and a money-lender is that the entrepreneur becomes a part of the venture whilst the role of the money-lender is purely to lend the money and collect their interest. Money-lenders require security, be it a mortgage on property or, in some medieval cases, on the whole country. The entrepreneur uses their resources (and the resources of others) with less tangible security and stands to fall if the venture fails. The money-lender can be fairly sure of their income, as the rate of interest will be set at the commencement of the loan. The entrepreneur uses the money to work for them in ventures but the result, be it profit or loss, may well be unknown. Whilst modern forecasting techniques are very sophisticated they do not always produce answers that are borne out in practice. Virgin predicted huge sales for its Virgin Cola product in the early 1990s and yet the product never really made a huge dent in the sales of either Coca-Cola or Pepsi Cola. Forecasts are not the same as customers putting their hands in their pockets.

As with any new enterprise, entrepreneurs must rely on instinct to a large degree. If one considers those entrepreneurs who began to finance the so-called voyages of discovery, instinct and belief played a large part in their lives. The Church preached that the Earth was flat and it was an offence (sometimes punishable by death) to state otherwise. Yet there were those who would help resource voyages that were clearly designed to go beyond "the edge of the world." The voyages of discovery were nothing of the sort. They only gained that title after the event. They were, in the main, voyages to seek new markets and new products. They were commercial rather than purely exploratory.

These voyages were often successful but many still ended in failure and the ship and its crew, paid for by entrepreneurs, were never seen again. The entrepreneur risked their money on the venture, rarely their life. The prospective explorer (whose motives may well have been purely exploration and knowledge) had to convince the entrepreneur of the feasibility and chances of commercial success for the venture. The entrepreneur would then provide resources, some of their own and some from others whom they would persuade to part with money, for the venture to take place. This is no different to the way Sir Richard Branson has been approached with ideas. If he deemed them worthy of a chance he went ahead and often sought other investors. Not much has changed save the financial scale of the ventures and a diminution in the possibilities of physical harm.

As peoples around the world began to circumnavigate it from about the fifteenth century onwards the opportunities for entrepreneurship grew. Trade is a process of exchange and entrepreneurs in Europe could send out a ship loaded with goods that would provide the basis for a venture by an entrepreneur in China who would in turn send silks to his counterpart in Europe. Still others went into the shipping industry itself where there was the danger of losses but huge profits to be made. Others built the ships, yet others acquired the forest for the wood to build the ships. Entrepreneurship is a network, hence the importance of building relationships.

The industrial revolution of the late eighteenth and into the nineteenth century produced huge opportunities for entrepreneurship. Innovation was moving faster than ever before. In 1800 there were no iron ships and the wooden vessels of the time were driven by the wind acting on sails save for a handful of experimental steam vessels. The first regular steamship operation between Europe and the US (as opposed to single voyages under steam) was that of a Canadian entrepreneur named Samuel Cunard who gained a UK mail contract in 1839 for a service between Liverpool and Boston (MA). His four original ships were 960 GRT (Gross Registered Tonnes – a measurement of the volume of the vessel and not its physical weight) and carried 63 passengers. The ships took eleven days to Halifax and a further three to Boston! In 1907 his company, now the mighty Cunard Line, launched the *Mauretania* of nearly 32,000 GRT carrying 2335 passengers and taking just four days from the UK to the US. The ship held the Atlantic record for the shortest crossing (the Blue Riband) from 1909 until 1924. Cunard's name still lives on today on the side of the *Queen Elizabeth II* but the brand is now owned by the US Carnival Group, the largest cruise company in the world.

Cunard was not the only entrepreneur to enter this potentially huge market. Emigration from Europe to the US was growing. In 1831 a German entrepreneur named Albert Ballin suggested to a Hamburg shipowner, Edward Carr, that he should adapt for the transportation of emigrants two freight ships he was having built. If he did this and charged only 75% of the fares of competitors, Ballin would assure him of customers. Ballin provided 11,000 emigrants in the first year and Carr expanded to six ships. The veteran Hamburg Amerika Line was damaged by this competition and in 1886 the two companies merged, and in 1899 Ballin was given the position of managing director and took the company into an expansion that was to last until 1914 when World War I broke out in Europe. By 1918 Hamburg Amerika was destroyed but was to rise again.

THE US CIVIL WAR

The end of the US Civil War in 1865 saw a huge expansion of commerce in the country and the rise of US entrepreneurism that began to assume global proportions. Whilst the exploration of North America had never entirely ceased, the years from 1865 saw the population moving out of the East and over the mighty Mississippi River in large numbers. The discovery of gold in California and the Dakotas brought migrants from the East and also from Asia. Whilst few became rich through finding gold, those who could provide the implements and entertainment that the prospectors required soon found that there was real money to be made. The West also provided new opportunities for agriculture with wide-open prairies and soon settlements were springing up all over.

Those entrepreneurs who became involved with the railroads began to resource the dream of linking the eastern and western US. Asa Whitney, a New York entrepreneur whose fortune had been made trading with China, was one of the first to suggest, as early as 1845, the linking of the two sides of the country by railroad. Cyrus Kurtz Holliday persuaded other investors to join him in setting up the Atchison and Topeka Railroad, later to become the famed Atchison, Topeka, and Santa Fé. James Jerome Hill, "the Empire Builder," was responsible for the Great Northern and the "big four," Leland Stamford, Mark Hopkins, Collis P. Huntington and Charles Croker, were building up a network that would become the Central Pacific. In 1862, during the Civil War, President Lincoln had signed the Pacific Railroad Act authorizing the Central Pacific to build from Sacramento (CA) to Promontory (UT) where it would meet the Union Pacific coming west from Omaha. On May 10, 1869 the two lines met and the US had a steel ribbon that joined the east and west coasts to form a continuous artery.

Further north, UK entrepreneurs and investors had provided money for the Canadian Pacific and in 1885 the two sides of Canada were joined. In this case there was an important political consideration as the governments in London and Ottawa feared that British Columbia would join the US if the railroad were not built.

These developments could not have occurred without entrepreneurs of vision who could see past the difficulties and then persuade others to invest. The investments paid off and soon the railroad companies were encouraging settlers to come to the towns that were springing up alongside the railroad. The entrepreneurial were there first, setting up shops, stables, saloons, barbers, newspapers, etc., and then reaping the rewards as populations grew.

It was now easier and easier for people to travel not only across the US but also from Europe to the West Coast. Huge liners would move them safely across the Atlantic to New York where famously-named trains such as the *20th Century Limited* would speed them to California in just a few days. They were unrivalled until the advent of the Boeing 707 and Douglas DC8 jet airliners in the 1950s provided such dramatic and speedy competition as to sound the death knell of the ocean liner as it was and the transcontinental railway. Both were to be resurrected by later entrepreneurs to cater for the tourist industry.

These developments also led to the great entrepreneurial combines, not least of which was the empire of J.P. Morgan. It is a little known fact that the infamous *Titanic*, well-known for sinking on her maiden voyage after colliding with an iceberg in April 1912, may well have flown the blue ensign (her captain was an officer in the Royal Naval Reserve and thus entitled to fly the blue and not the red ensign), and was officered and crewed almost entirely by UK citizens, was registered in Liverpool and owned by the apparently British White Star Line, but was in fact owned by a US entrepreneur and financier – J.P. Morgan and the Morgan Guarantee Trust. Morgan had acquired interests in White Star and a number of other UK and European shipping lines and had tried to buy Cunard until thwarted by the UK government. He was helped in his acquisition by the chairman of the Harland & Wolff shipbuilders in Belfast, William (later Lord) Pirrie. Harland & Wolff built all of White Star's ships including the *Titanic*'s two sisters, the *Olympic*, which had a long and successful career, and the *Britannic*, sunk in World War I whilst serving as a hospital ship. Morgan's ambition appears to have been to develop a monopoly on the lucrative North Atlantic passenger trade and it should be noted that he was heavily involved in railroad developments and financing in the US.

The loss of the *Titanic* and subsequent losses in World War I denied him his ambition but it is interesting to note that few on either side of the Atlantic were aware that a US entrepreneur had acquired no fewer than five UK and one Belgian shipping companies, including White Star and its large fleet of passenger liners. When the UK government realized that as a maritime nation part of its strategic reserve was under the control of a foreigner, it acted immediately to subsidize Cunard (hence the building of the *Mauretania* – see earlier – and the *Lusitania*). Part of the subsidy was a requirement that Cunard must remain British, a condition not changed until Carnival (started by the US entrepreneur Ted Arison in 1972 with one ship and now the largest cruise company in the world) acquired the Cunard brand and ships in 1998.

The growth of the middle classes and increased disposable income after 1918 led to more and more opportunities for entrepreneurs and a whole new area of business for them to expand into – that of aircraft. The primitive machines of the Wright Brothers had grown to become multi-engined Goliaths during the course of the war and it was not long before aircraft designers and entrepreneurs were coming together to form manufacturing plants and airlines. Information about the partnerships between the inventors, designers, and entrepreneurs can be found in *Destination Disaster* by Paul Eddy, Elaine Potter and Bruce Page, who also provide a useful insight into the funding of multi-million dollar enterprises.

It was not only travel that was providing opportunities for entrepreneurial activity. Entertainment and domestic products, including radios, the beginnings of television, motion pictures, washing machines, refrigerators, etc., were in demand. New methods of selling, advertising and delivery were being tried. At the end of the nineteenth century mail order through organizations such as Sears had brought mainstream products out to settlers wherever they were in the US. Bigger and bigger department stores were being built. Isidor Straus and his brother had approached the owners of R.H. Macy in New York for a corner of the new store in which to sell glass and chinaware. In 10 years they owned Macy's in New York and eventually over 80 stores nationwide. In a link with J.P. Morgan, the 135 W34th St. entrance to Macy's in New York is known as the Memorial Entrance, for Isidor Straus' wife who refused to be parted from him one cold night in April 1912; witnesses reported how they calmly sat down together on the boat deck of the *SS Titanic*, preferring to die as they had lived – together. They were both senior citizens at the time.

POST WORLD WAR II

It might be thought that the period post-1945 that has seen the growth of huge global organizations might have provided fewer opportunities for individual entrepreneurship. The opposite has actually been the case. Huge organizations may not always be prepared to take even calculated risks on brand new developments, preferring to let others take the chances and then buy them out if they are successful. There are also many niche markets that larger organizations are less interested in and that can still provide a good living to a smaller operator.

The development of consumer electronics and then computers has provided a host of opportunity for new, often quite young, entrepreneurs. (As mentioned earlier in this material, both Gates and Branson were still at high school when they began their entrepreneurial activities.) The "dot com" companies that began to spring up in the late 1990s were the product of some very young, fertile, and entrepreneurial minds and it is likely that this pattern will continue.

Every age will throw up opportunities and it is the entrepreneurial who will reach out and grasp them. Where next? – biotechnology, space, who knows?

TIME-LINE

Due to the generic nature and long time-period of the subject, the time-line in Fig. 3.2 illustrates the major focus of entrepreneurial activities at particular periods in history.

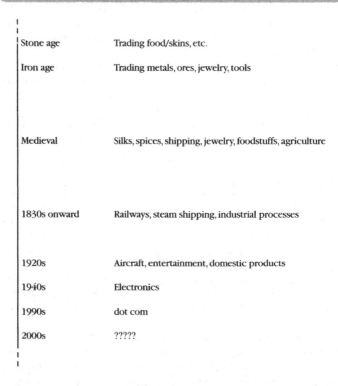

Stone age	Trading food/skins, etc.
Iron age	Trading metals, ores, jewelry, tools
Medieval	Silks, spices, shipping, jewelry, foodstuffs, agriculture
1830s onward	Railways, steam shipping, industrial processes
1920s	Aircraft, entertainment, domestic products
1940s	Electronics
1990s	dot com
2000s	?????

Fig. 3.2 Time-line: major focus of entrepreneurial activity throughout history.

KEY LEARNING POINTS

» Inventors, discoverers, and explorers need entrepreneurs and entrepreneurs need inventors, discoverers, and explorers. They are complementary to each other.
» Entrepreneurship is a normal part of human behavior.
» Once trade starts, entrepreneurship is always right behind.

Implications of the Internet for the Entrepreneurial Individual

The Internet provides opportunities for a number of forms of entrepreneurship. These include:

- » opportunities for the entrepreneur to offer Internet-related products;
- » new forms of advertising, communications, and information;
- » new opportunities for the sale and delivery of non-Internet related products;
- » it is not necessary for an entrepreneur to understand the Internet in detail but they do need the vision and ideas to see how the Internet can add value to their products and services;

» size of organization is irrelevant when considering the implications of the Internet for the entrepreneurial individual; and
» the Internet makes geography and distance much less relevant to the relationship between the entrepreneur and their customer base.

The rapid growth in the use of the Internet during the latter part of the 1990s provided huge opportunities for entrepreneurial activity. The Internet became a means by which young, technically-minded entrepreneurs could find a market niche for themselves, but that does not preclude the older, less technically-adept from using the Internet to further their business vision.

WHAT CAN THE INTERNET OFFER?

Basically the Internet is a network of linked computers that can be accessed from any remote site using another computer and a modem. All kinds of information can be placed on the computers of the network. These servers hold the information in the form of Web pages, each with its URL (Uniform Resource Locator) that can be opened either by anybody or by specified people in possession of a password. Users of the Internet do not even have to know the URL as there are a number of search engines such as Lycos, Yahoo!, Excite, etc., that will search the Internet for a user and find all the sites that match the keywords that they have been requested to find.

There are thus a number of ways that the Internet can impact on entrepreneurial activity:

» it provides opportunities for the entrepreneur to offer Internet-related products;
» it is a new form of advertising, communications, and information medium; and
» it offers new opportunities for the sale and delivery of non-Internet related products.

INTERNET-RELATED PRODUCTS

Any new form of technology, whether it is the steam engine or the computer, soon generates a market for ancillary products. For example, as soon as railways began to move people over long distances, passengers had to be fed. Individual entrepreneurs began to offer lunch hampers. The UK-born US entrepreneur Fred Harvey was not a steam engineer but he saw a market in providing eating-houses at major stations, his first in Topeka, being followed by 53 more. They were staffed by young ladies, 20,000 of whom out of the 100,000 employed ended up marrying customers. Given the shortage of suitable wives in the West at the time, Harvey's entrepreneurship served another purpose. The menus were arranged so that on a long journey the traveler would have different choices at each stop. J.D. Porterfield states in *Dining by Rail* (1993) that Harvey was the first of the fast food entrepreneurs, beginning a trend that has continued with Macdonald's, Burger King, Kentucky Fried Chicken, etc. Harvey saw a niche in the growing railroad market and moved to fill it.

To make the most use of the Internet, the entrepreneur will need search engines and a Website. Entrepreneurs such as Bob Davis – Lycos; Jerry Yang – Yahoo!; Jim Barksdale – Netscape; Rod Schrock – AltaVista; and Steve and Tina Medin – imageData (see case study at the end of this chapter) have all provided products that ease the use of the Internet for ordinary users in the same way as Harvey provided a service both for the railroad company and its passengers, saving the former from having to set up a catering operation but being able to claim that Harvey added value to their core transportation product.

Christopher Price has profiled the entrepreneurial activities of many of the new Internet entrepreneurs in his book, *The Internet Entrepreneurs* (2000). As he points out, many of the companies had not made anything but losses up to 2000. Indeed, as he states, the combined losses by the 13 entrepreneurs he considered had reached $4bn by 1999 but the value of their companies was considered to be in the region of $170bn. It is hardly surprising that a new technology had not produced profits as it is necessary to wait whilst market share builds up before profits occur. This is not a new phenomenon. The *Titanic* has been mentioned earlier. Gardiner and Van der Vat in *The Riddle of the Titanic* (1995) calculated that her sister, *Olympic*, needed to work hard for at least six years before she repaid her building costs. Entrepreneurs and venture capitalists need patience and stamina. As Price states, it is hard to lose money, especially other people's, with only self-belief to keep one going. However, all of his Internet entrepreneurs appear to have had no shortage of either self-belief or vision. Sooner or later they believed it would all come good. The value of Internet companies slumped from 2000 onwards not, perhaps, because of a fundamental flaw in the product but because investors began to realize that it would take time for the public to adapt to using the Net in the same way they used other retail outlets.

The supply of Internet-related products is currently still very early in the product life cycle. It is characteristic of the early product life cycle stages for there to be a large number of suppliers of similar products. Later there will be a phase known as shake-out where mergers occur. This is beginning to happen; the abortive deal between Davis' Lycos and Diller's USA Networks in 1999 and its eventual sale to a Spanish company, Terra Networks, in 2000, plus the AOL (America On Line) link-up with Time Warner, are evidence of shake-out starting.

Eventually the new Internet-related companies will either become mature players in their own right or will be acquired by bigger names. By that time, however, their entrepreneurial founders will probably have moved on to start newer ventures at the cutting edge.

A NEW FORM OF ADVERTISING, COMMUNICATIONS, AND INFORMATION MEDIUM

The letterheads for more and more of even the smallest organizations now bear a "www" Web address. As customers become more and more used to using the Internet as a serious research and information tool as opposed to a novelty, it would be a brave organization that decided to ignore the huge potential customer base that the Net can reach.

In the next section it will be noted that kilt-makers in Scotland regularly take orders form the US over the Net and the Vermont Teddy Bear Company in the US will supply teddy bears all over the world; just click on their Website. Flowers, books, in fact almost anything can be found on the Web.

Data for serious and not-so-serious research is there in abundance. In 1999 it was reported that a US couple wishing to relocate to the UK logged on to a UK CCTV (Closed Circuit Television) camera in a town center location and so liked what they saw of the lifestyle that they purchased a house in the town.

Every major corporation and government agency has Web pages full of statistics, many of which are available without charge. Terminals for searching the Web are in libraries and Internet cafés the world over. As a communications medium using electronic mail (e-mail) and a form of advertising the Web is quick and interactive. Customer comments can be received and acted upon far quicker than by letter.

Search engine entrepreneurs can also use this facet of the Web. As Jerry Yang, the entrepreneur responsible for Yahoo!, has asked "how can a search engine make money, will users pay for it?" The answer is that they won't, but advertisers will pay for inclusion on the site. The advertising banners on Web pages and search engines may be annoying at times but it is their presence that allows for free access once payment has been made to the ISP (Internet Service Provider). One difficulty that the providers of search engines may find is that it would now be almost impossible to charge for the service as the world is so used to it being free.

SALE AND DELIVERY OF NON-INTERNET RELATED PRODUCTS

One of the most well-known organizations using the Internet for business is Amazon.com, founded by the US entrepreneur Jeff Bezos, featured as a case study in *Going Global*, another title in the *ExpressExec* series. Whilst Amazon.com may use the latest in Internet technology for its sales effort, the product is a very old one – books. Amazon.com is a virtual bookshop (now also selling CDs, etc.) operating on an almost global basis using new technology to make buying an established product easier. Bezos may be one of the best known entrepreneurs in the new way of selling an old product field, but he is not alone. As will be shown in Chapter 5, when considering globalization, the fact that the Internet does not conform to national boundaries allows even the smallest organization to become global using just a computer, an ISP (AOL, Freeserve, CompuServe, btnet, etc.), a modem, and access to a postal or courier service.

There is very little that cannot be bought on the Internet. Small retailers can reach a global market. One can buy cars, houses, teddy bears from Vermont, and kilts and salmon from Scotland without leaving home. The only customer resistance is in the areas of not being able to touch the product and concerns about the security of the monetary transaction. The latter problem is being solved as systems become more and more secure.

This form of business is just an update of the mail order pioneered by companies such as Sears to supply settlers during the expansion of the US in the nineteenth and early twentieth centuries.

Importantly for the entrepreneur, he or she does not have to be technologically adept. All that is required is the vision to see the possibilities. There are plenty of other entrepreneurs who will design and maintain the Internet site (see imageData Corp.) at the end of this chapter. It is rare to find any business of any size today that does not have its own Website, so important is this form of information and advertising becoming.

Jay Walker's Priceline operation that matches buyers, sellers, and the price the former are prepared to pay, is an imaginative use of the Net. Commencing with airline tickets on two US airlines, a buyer could say "I wish to fly from Denver to LA on Monday or Tuesday next and I am prepared to pay $75." Airlines usually have spare seats and it might well be that one of the participating carriers would accept this deal on a lightly-loaded flight provided that the offer was over the marginal cost. The operation has since expanded to include more airlines, hotels, and car hire companies. The immediacy of the Web makes this possible. Priceline gets a commission and that is the way the company earns revenue.

BEST PRACTICE

imageData

This case study deliberately takes a small organization involved in the Internet as an example that entrepreneurial activities start small and grow.

Steve and Tina Medin started imageData in 1994 as a technology consultancy assisting corporations with database-driven applications that increased workforce productivity. As with many high-tech entrepreneurs their first premises were also domestic – a spare bedroom. Their work soon expanded to include Internet technologies and the creation of dynamic data-driven Websites. In 2000 they moved into their own offices.

Steve Medin began his career as a programmer for a large financial software company, McCormack & Dodge, at the time a subsidiary of Dun & Bradstreet Corporation. From there he took a position with CSC Partners, a computer sciences corporation, where he applied his technical skills to consulting engagements at the corporate offices of *Fortune 500* companies, such as Sara Lee and the Pepsi Corporation. In 1994 he decided to work on his own and formed imageData as his own technology consultancy, with an eye towards growing the firm into a Web design and hosting business. He is currently managing imageData's hosting operations as well as programming and database design services for clients. He also provides on-site consulting services as a system architect for a large Internet security firm located in Needham (MA).

Tina met Steve at McCormack & Dodge in 1986. Her role was to provide support for their purchasing and invoice-matching software, and to conduct customer product training classes. Five years later the company merged with its competitor, Management Software of Atlanta (MSA), and corporate headquarters moved to Georgia. Wishing to remain in the North East Corridor she then took a position as an installation specialist with Collaborative Medical Systems, a medical software company that served the information management needs of hospital pathology and cytology laboratories. Several years later she joined Steve in his efforts to develop the Web design and hosting business, applying her project management, client support, and training experience to developing an approach to marketing imageData's services and a methodology for developing commercial Websites.

imageData are situated in Waltham (MA) just outside Boston. Waltham is also the headquarters of Lycos (see earlier) so the town is no stranger to high-tech innovation. Whilst California and Silicon Valley may have Stanford on the doorstep, Waltham has both Harvard and MIT (Massachusetts Institute of Technology).

Both Tina and Steve seek to provide a customer-driven service for Web design and hosting, a service where the client is in control and they provide the expertise. They both believe in working in partnership with their growing client list which includes Boston IVF, Jeepers, and Swagbag. They also provide an on-line guide to membrane switches for the ITC (Information Technology and Communications) industry, indeed it is the only comprehensive list available in the US.

Their process of developing a client relationship is as follows.

» They create the navigational prototype of the client's site, based on the site structure agreed upon in their design proposal. This navigational model reflects the overall structure of the site and the path visitors will take through the pages. When the navigational model is complete, it will be submitted for client discussion and review.
» After approval of the navigational model, they develop a graphical prototype of the Website using graphics provided by the client or creating new ones utilizing images from their extensive library of clip-art and royalty-free photographs to create logos, backgrounds, navigation objects, and other accents.
» Typically developed by the client, content is the information contained in the Website. While imageData offer copy-writing services, more often than not the client has marketing literature and product information to draw upon that can be utilized in the Web page design. Content may be presented "as is" or segmented throughout appropriate pages on the site.

Steve and Tina Medin have the philosophy that working with imageData is like having expert Web designers and Internet professionals on the organization's payroll, without the associated personnel, software, and hardware costs. imageData staff will work closely with the organization as its Website design and Internet technology specialists. They stress the importance of listening to the client and understanding the client's business, industry sector, marketing goals, and strategies.

They are proud to share their expertise, assisting to educate clients about the Web as a global market-place and technological arena. Questions are answered in plain English, not jargon. This is an important point. Entrepreneurs need to remember that their customers may not share their enthusiasm for technology and may be put off by too much jargon.

imageData also offer a monitored 24-hours-a-day, 7-days-a-week, 365-days-a-year hosting service to ensure that, whenever someone wants to access a client Website, it will be there.

Goals

According to the Medins, their goal is "to develop a Web presentation for clients that will be an accurate reflection of the client's organization company: professional, efficient, and effective."

That is why they do not offer Web design "packages," where the designer offers a specific number of pages with limitations on graphics and links. While the simplicity is enticing, it can carry hidden costs. As they state, "We won't force you to squeeze your size 11 feet into a size 9 shoe."

As imageData tell clients:

» for a fraction of the cost of running a quarter-page ad in a local newspaper, they can have a Web presentation that will reach millions of prospects around the world, 24 hours a day, 7 days a week;

» for a fraction of the cost of sales materials and direct mailings, they can have a Website where their customers and staff can have access to the organization's best sales presentation at any time, from anywhere in the world;

» for a fraction of the cost of employee education and training, they can have an "intranet" Website to communicate the latest information about the organization and products to staff, whether they are in the office, on the road, or working in overseas offices; and

» the World Wide Web eliminates geographic and cultural boundaries and opens the door to the world for clients.

When Steve and Tina Medin started what has become imageData, Web design was a fairly new thing. As such, there really weren't many business models to emulate. In 1994–5 clients were very naive and uncertain of exactly what could be gained from investing their marketing dollars in this "new technology." Many were skeptical that the Internet as an advertising medium would yield an adequate return on investment. Their biggest challenge at that time was convincing some prospects that a Website would become as common a marketing tool as a brochure. A URL became somewhat of a "vanity plate" or status symbol for smaller companies seeking to compete in national or global arenas. Small companies embraced the idea of a "level playing field" where they could, for not a lot of money, look as sleek and professional as their much larger competitors.

In 1994-5 the industry was still immature, and there were very few standards among Web designers, since many of them, including the Medins, were learning as they went along. Clients couldn't distinguish whether they were dealing with a large company or an individual, since just about everyone in the business was a neophyte to some degree. As the technology matured and designers became more savvy, so did the clients. Websites began to become more than just "brochureware," evolving into a tool to minimize repetitive administrative tasks and facilitate the easy flow of information between organizations and their customers while reducing workload on their staff.

Today typical clients are much more technology-literate, and often approach imageData with their own ideas of what they would like their Website to do for them and for their customers. As a result, interactions with prospects have evolved from "Hey, look what you can do with this!" to "We understand what you want to do and here is how we would do it." Whilst Steve and Tina (and their growing staff) adhere to the same principle of not "baffling with jargon," they also have to recognize that their clients' level of technical knowledge has grown since the "good old days," and they need to be careful not to be perceived as underestimating the client's intelligence. They have seen a significant shift in the client's desire to master the lingo and challenge imageData's knowledge of Internet technology with some jargon of their own.

Whilst imageData may be small, it is an example of how two entrepreneurs starting from a home-based business can grow that business by listening to the customer and offering the customer a product tailored to their needs. The experience of Steve and Tina Medin shows that small organizations can become really close to their customers (see Chapter 6) and can offer the same high standards as much larger organizations. For contact details on imageData please see Chapter 9.

KEY LEARNING POINTS

» The Internet can give individual entrepreneurs with the vision to use it creatively a chance to compete with larger organizations as it diminishes geographic and distance effects.

» As with imageData, individual entrepreneurs can be successful in technology especially if they work closely with clients to demystify the technology – this may be harder for larger organizations to achieve.

» The entrepreneur does not have to be a technological expert to make use of the Internet; expertise can be bought-in, vision cannot.

The Individual Entrepreneur and the Global Dimension

» The entrepreneurial individual starting a new venture is likely to begin in a small local manner.
» There are global factors such as exchange rates, etc., that even the most locally-based entrepreneur cannot ignore.
» Modern technology means that competition may come from other parts of the world to affect the most locally-based entrepreneurial activity.
» If the entrepreneur has a tourist-related product or service, simple customer enhancements can aid competitive advantage.
» Once an entrepreneur, always an entrepreneur.
» Whilst the present may be local, the dream and the future may be global.

The entrepreneurial individual starting out on a new venture probably has no more than a local, regional, or national focus. He or she may have dreams of being a global player but it is nearly always necessary to build up a loyal local customer base before considering any form of expansion beyond national borders. This does not mean, however, that the entrepreneur should ignore the global dimension.

Bryan *et al.* (*Race for the World* (1999) – see Chapter 9) calculated that by 2000 20% of world output would be produced and consumed in global markets and that by 2030 the figure could be as high as 80%. As was shown in the previous chapter, Internet developments are breaking down geographic and political boundaries. Some products and brands are now truly global, a point continued in more detail in *Going Global*, companion material in the *ExpressExec* series.

Coca-Cola, Ford, Shell, Microsoft, Sony, to name but five, are global brands. Whilst three have US origins, one (Shell) is from the Netherlands (the full name of the company is Royal Dutch Shell) and Sony is Japanese, they all operate in a global market and actually belong to where their customers are. This point was introduced in *Managing Diversity*, another title in the *ExpressExec* series, when considering the success of Coca-Cola. By building complete production and distribution facilities in different countries, Coca-Cola became associated with both that country and the US – it is a semi-indigenous product.

If the above figures are correct it means that much of the competition in the world will be global rather than local and this leaves the entrepreneurial individual with a difficult decision – is what they propose good enough to compete globally? Even if the answer is no, all is not lost. Christopher Price in *The Internet Entrepreneurs* states that "niches are for wimps." The writer of this material begs to differ. Local/regional niches may be a very attractive place for an entrepreneur who can use local knowledge and a close relationship to their customers to compete with a much larger organization. Towns and villages throughout the world are full of small-scale operations that can compete in niche areas that are deemed too small to interest the huge, global players.

GLOBAL ISSUES THAT HAVE IMPLICATIONS FOR THE INDIVIDUAL ENTREPRENEUR

Exchange rates

No matter how local the initial or future operations of an individual entrepreneur are, exchange rates will have implications for the financial affairs of their operation. Exchange rates tend to be affected by both national and international factors and can affect the price of supplies and especially oil. There are few, if any, business ventures that will be unaffected by a change in the price of oil.

The economies of the world are irrevocably bound up with the price of oil, given the importance of oil as the major fuel source for transportation and electricity generation. Whatever the entrepreneur does, the prices charged for a product or service will reflect, in some part, the cost of energy and thus the cost of oil. In some areas where oil is relatively cheap or there are alternate energy supplies, the proportionate effect will be smaller but it will always be present to some degree or other. Even the cost of food will need to reflect the energy costs of producing and transporting the product.

Those who need supplies from abroad will also need to pay for those supplies in either local currency or (as is becoming the case in many developing economies) the US dollar.

The adoption of a common currency to replace national currencies completely (the Euro – €) by 12 EU (European Union) members from January 2002 will have considerable effects on individual entrepreneurs in those countries. Interest rates for Eurozone countries are set by the European Central Bank in Frankfurt and are the same for all 12 members. This is one of the stated reasons for the reluctance of the UK to adopt the Euro, as a number of politicians believe that it will remove sovereignty by restricting the management of national economies. In the UK (as in the US where they are set by the Federal Reserve) interest rates were set by the government but from 1997 onwards this has been the task of the independent Bank of England.

Economic and political groupings

The world appears to be moving towards a situation where individual economies are bound ever closer together in economic and political unions. Perhaps the most advanced along this road is the EU but NAFTA (North American Free Trade Agreement) is also an important force in world economics containing as it does the US economy.

Entrepreneurs in EU member countries have to obey not only the commercial and employment laws of their own countries but also those of the EU. EU law is superior to national law and thus issues such as working times and conditions set in Brussels and Strasbourg will have implications for business owners and managers across the EU. The EU Social Charter, the format for which was agreed in 1989, provides for a comprehensive harmonization of social and employment policy throughout the EU. The UK did not sign up for the Charter until the election of the Labour government in 1997 but is now a full signatory. As Richard Pettinger, in *The European Social Charter* (1998), has stated, the Charter is designed to protect EU citizens against varying standards of social conditions and employment practices and thus forms part of the move towards harmonization across the EU.

Entrepreneurs and all in business in the EU cannot avoid a consideration of EU policy and legislation when making decisions, especially as the EU has also legislated on competition. The so-called "trade wars" between the EU and the US, brought about by disagreements over the GATT agreement (General Agreement on Tariffs and Trade), have had implications for a wide range of commercial sectors as protectionist policies on both sides have been deployed against products that are not themselves the subject of any disagreement. At one stage it was believed that the US would place tariffs on Scottish cashmere products in retaliation for the EU policy on bananas from the Caribbean!

Foreign competition

In the previous chapter it was noted that the Internet has removed many of the barriers posed by geography and distance. If an entrepreneur in location A can penetrate market B, then their competitor in B can also sell to A. Competition is a two-way process. One of the issues of Japanese expansion in the 1970s and 80s was the reluctance of the Japanese to import goods from areas they were supplying with considerable levels of Japanese products. Such an imbalance nearly always leads to the threat of quota impositions to assist in redressing the balance.

Global supplies

More and more supplies are being obtained from further and further away from the user. Entrepreneurs will always want the best deal possible. There may be very good "political" reasons for sourcing supplies locally – it can generate excellent, often free, publicity. Nevertheless, some supplies and services may be much cheaper abroad. Data processing has become a speciality in India where labor costs are lower than in Europe or the US. Modern communications technology means that data can flow down telephone lines and along satellite links at the speed of light, rendering the physical distance irrelevant.

The entrepreneurial individual should assess all the supply options available in order to balance cost and quality. The less spent on supplies, provided that the minimum quality required is maintained, may mean more profit to reinvest in the project.

Whilst there may well be currency exchange issues these are not likely to deter an entrepreneur.

The very act of buying supplies abroad may provide the entrepreneur with an entry into and contacts in the market in that area, a considerable spin-off possibility.

Global sales

The ability of the Internet to break down geographic barriers was covered in the previous chapter. There is growing anecdotal evidence that tourists, whilst on vacation, who have purchased items abroad from those with the entrepreneurial foresight to have equipped their operation with a Website and credit card facilities, may well not only make repeat purchases when they return home but may generate further business through their friends, colleagues, and relatives.

Tourism

Tourism is a global multi-billion dollar industry. Those who can meet the wants and needs of tourists can do very well. Meeting the requirements of tourists requires the entrepreneur to research the likely market very carefully. There are a number of simple actions that the entrepreneurial can take to gain the necessary competitive advantage over their rivals, most of which cost very little indeed:

» provide signs in other languages;
» provide information material in other languages;
» accept foreign currency, especially US dollars;
» provide information about and directions to other local attractions;
» understand and provide food and drink that the tourist requires;
» extend opening times to suit those touring for whom time may be precious;
» arrange sending and delivery for large items; and
» provide e-mail access for visitors.

The above are fairly simple and yet likely to be very welcome to potential tourist customers.

A NEW START

Some people's extreme misfortune can be the start of an opportunity for the entrepreneurial individual. One has only to look at the number of successful US businesses founded by those from Korea and Vietnam or the entrepreneurial activities in the UK of some of the East African Asians expelled from their homes by Kenya and Uganda in the 1960s and 70s. Many of these people who arrived in the US and UK with nothing other than their personal possessions were highly successful in their former lives. They did not sit around hoping for something to turn up. They began being entrepreneurial again in a small way and many have grown highly successful businesses. A new start is always possible. Perhaps once an entrepreneur, always an entrepreneur.

THE FUTURE

One of the points already made in this material is the need for entrepreneurs to have vision. There is no reason at all why the entrepreneurial individual should not have a vision that stretches beyond the immediate geographic area.

In the modern world it is certainly necessary to know and understand what overseas competitors might be doing to break into one's own area and, once a local base has been established and a reputation gained, then why not think about expanding into the wider world? Entrepreneurship needs a dream and dreams can be unlimited.

BEST PRACTICE
Yahoo!

Some of the research for this material was conducted using the Internet and the World Wide Web. To do that, as mentioned in Chapter 4, requires the use of a search engine. Almost by definition a search engine for the World Wide Web has to be global. The search engine is linked to the engine's database (in this case the Yahoo! database) containing the addresses of all the Web pages that have been registered with it. Most organizations register their Web pages with all of the major search engines, Yahoo!, Lycos, AltaVista, Excite, etc.

Yahoo! began as a scientific hobby. The two developers of Yahoo!, David Filo and Jerry Yang, doctoral candidates in electrical engineering at Stanford University in California, started their guide to the World Wide Web in April 1994 as a way to keep track of their personal interests on the Internet. Before long they found that their lists were becoming too long and unwieldy. Gradually they began to spend more and more time on the search engine that became Yahoo!

During 1994 they converted Yahoo! into a customized database designed to serve the needs of the thousands of users who began to use the service through the closely-bound academic and Internet communities both in the US and abroad. They therefore developed software to help them efficiently locate, identify, and edit material stored on the Internet. The name Yahoo! is supposed to stand for "Yet Another Hierarchical Officious Oracle" but Filo and Yang insist they selected the name because they considered themselves Yahoos. The Yahoo! database first resided on Yang's student workstation while the search engine was lodged on Filo's computer.

In 1995 Filo and Yang were invited to move their files over to larger computers housed at Netscape Communications. Today's commercial version of Yahoo! contains organized information on tens of thousands of computers linked to the Web. Yahoo! reports that *The San José Mercury* news noted that "Yahoo! is closest in spirit to the work of Linnaeus, the eighteenth century botanist whose classification system organized the natural world.''

The fact that from early on Yahoo! was used by those not in the US has meant a rapid global growth for the organization. As an example, there are Yahoo! organizational offices and Internet access in Denmark, France, Germany, Italy, Norway, Spain, Sweden, UK/Eire, Australia, New Zealand, China/Hong Kong, India, Japan, Singapore, South Korea, Taiwan, Argentina, Brazil, Canada, Mexico, and of course the US (where the sites can be accessed in Spanish or Chinese).

This is rapid but necessary growth. Many users may suspect that Yahoo! originated in the US, but with the Internet that does not matter. Provided that one can access local and global sites in one's own language, the point of origin of the facilitatory search engine does not matter at all.

Yahoo! is no longer a hobby but a global organization that shows what can be possible in a very short time, given a couple of entrepreneurs and a vision.

KEY LEARNING POINTS

» Entrepreneurial activities usually start on a local basis.
» The right product, however, such as Yahoo!, may grow into a global operation very quickly.
» Even the most local entrepreneur has to analyze and be prepared for global factors that may impact on operations. These may often be financial or legal.
» An entrepreneurial individual is often quite capable of starting again from scratch following a setback.

The State of the Art of Individual Entrepreneurship

The key skills, attributes, and areas that an entrepreneurial individual must develop and take account of are as follows.

Attributes:
» vision
» commitment
» self-belief
» discipline
» risk-taking
» concern for the customer
» creativity.

Skills:
» analysis
» networking
» building relationships
» negotiation
» selling
» finance.

Plus:
» a consideration of occupational roles;
» keeping a healthy body and a healthy mind;
» retaining the support of the family; and
» making time for family relationships.

Part of the discipline required for the entrepreneurial individual is time management and the ability to delegate.

In Chapter 2 a list of the attributes and skills required for individual entrepreneurship was introduced.

Attributes:

» vision
» commitment
» self-belief
» discipline
» risk-taking
» concern for the customer
» creativity.

Skills:

» analysis
» networking
» building relationships
» negotiation
» selling
» finance.

The material in this chapter will examine each of these in turn. When reading this material you should ask yourself to what degree you currently possess these factors and how can you develop them.

Whilst some may feel that attributes are fixed, in reality we all probably possess the necessary ones to some degree. Self-knowledge can allow an individual to see how they can develop and grow what they have into what they need. Skills can be learnt – something we all do as children.

THE ATTRIBUTES NEEDED BY THE ENTREPRENEURIAL INDIVIDUAL

Vision

Everybody, it seems, who has ever commented on entrepreneurship mentions vision. Without vision it is impossible to be an entrepreneur. Bill Gates has it, Sir Richard Branson has it, Steve and Tina Medin (see Chapter 4) have it; all entrepreneurs have it.

Vision could be described as a dream with direction. The visionary not only dreams about something, they almost experience it in real time. A dream is experienced, a vision is lived in.

William Heinecke says that entrepreneurs should "set goals but go easy on the vision thing." Setting goals is important but without vision the daring steps are never taken. As this author has written when considering customer relations (*Mastering Customer Relations* [2000]), goals and objectives should be C-SMART:

» Customer-centered
» Specific
» Measurable
» Agreed
» Realistic
» Timely.

Vision can be individual entrepreneur-centered as long as it is then translated into a customer-centered approach to business. Indeed, vision is individual. One of the hardest things an entrepreneur has to do is to communicate their vision to others in such a way as to fire enthusiasm.

Vision does not have to be realistic – it needs to push back borders and it certainly does not need to be agreed with anybody, save your own imagination.

The entrepreneurial individual or potential entrepreneurial individual needs to ask themselves, "What is it I want from life, not just in financial, but in social, cultural, family, etc., terms?" Once that is articulated they can begin to build a vision around those ideas.

Vision, however, does need to be focussed on something tangible. There is no use in having the vision that you want to be the most successful person in the world, this is far too broad. As Heinecke also points out quite rightly when discussing vision, Bill Gates did not set out to be fabulously wealthy, his vision was the best software program in the world. That vision was focussed and could be worked towards in a systematic manner.

Entrepreneurs do not work alone. They need others around them to assist in their projects and they need external people for venture capital, financing, supplies, etc. Mark Peterson in *The Complete Entrepreneur*

(1996) has stated the importance of a good relationship with bankers and any employees one has. They need to have the vision communicated to them in terms they can understand. Bankers tend to be rather hard-headed and, whilst the entrepreneur may have flowing phrases for their vision, the bankers will want to hear about cash flow, revenue, and gearing. Employees will want to know about salaries, security, and lunch breaks. Vision operates on two planes, emotional and practical, and the successful entrepreneur phrases the vision in both.

Finally, it should be obvious that vision without all the other attributes and skills that are to be covered in this chapter cannot move the individual or their ideas forward. Committed hard work is required to make any vision a reality. It is hard to find an entrepreneur who does not continue working hard after they have made it (whatever it is for them) – entrepreneurship appears addictive!

Commitment

Commitment means hard work and an approach to the business that borders on obsession.

The entrepreneur must be prepared to commit to their vision. They must commit in the sunshine and the rain, on the really good days and on the awful ones. Commitment is the fuel to take the project or business to the vision.

One of the most reported facts about well-known entrepreneurs is their long working day and the difficulties their families have in persuading them to take a break. As will be shown in Chapter 7, when Sir Richard Branson goes on holiday it may be to Necker in the Caribbean but it may also be to fly over an ocean or round the globe in a balloon – hardly a relaxing vacation but it is something different and, like the buzz of business, is likely to have the adrenaline flowing.

Entrepreneurs are what is known as "type A" – fast burners ("type B" are much more laid back). Entrepreneurs need to be on the go, they must be involved, they must be doing something. If this is not you then entrepreneurship is probably not for you either. It is difficult to imagine a laid back entrepreneur.

The commitment of the entrepreneurial individual must be long term. Patience and tenacity are needed to see a business or project through to success. There will be failures as well as successes and it is an important part of self-belief (see next section) to be able to deal with both. As Kipling wrote in his famous poem *If* – "... if you can meet with Triumph and Disaster and treat those two impostors both the same ..." (the complete verse is quoted in Chapter 10). Failure should not lead to giving up but to learning lessons and there should be no complacency or diminution of commitment when success occurs. Success is the platform for moving on to the next challenge.

Self-belief

Entrepreneurial individuals believe in themselves. Not only that, they also possess another linked attribute that makes self-belief work: they know their limitations.

Self-belief requires success to sustain it, which begs the question, how can success be guaranteed? One method of making success as certain as possible is a technique known to teachers all over the world and is that of "chunking." By dividing a task up into a series of smaller steps, it is more likely that a series of small successes will occur. Chunking takes longer but as success tends to breed further success it is often well worth the extra time.

Within the overall vision, a series of goals can be set, success in one leading to work on the next, and so on. By chunking in this way confidence and self-belief can be built up. Those with hobbies usually know all about chunking. Model railroaders do not start with very expensive brass kits, they buy ready-to-run proprietary models, then a simple boxcar or wagon kit in plastic, then maybe a white metal locomotive kit of simple design, etc., working their way up to the complex brass models. Gardeners start with a small patch, not a stately home. Entrepreneurs should be the same. Start small and in stages and work up with each success.

Knowing one's limitations is also very important. The person who knows their limitations will not try to accomplish something they know that they cannot achieve success at until they have acquired some new skills or resources. This does not mean that they give up. If the task is important to the vision they will go out and either acquire the skills or resources for themselves or find somebody who can help.

Discipline

The entrepreneurial individual is there for the long term and that requires a considerable degree of self-discipline.

Entrepreneurship requires focussed effort and that requires discipline with human, physical, financial, and time resources. Nothing should be wasted, especially time.

The financial skills required by the entrepreneurial individual are covered later in this chapter but it requires discipline to not spend profits but to plough them back into the business and its projects. It also requires discipline (plus the self-belief and vision covered earlier in this chapter) to carry on putting financial resources into something that is losing money. As Christopher Price has pointed out in *The Internet Entrepreneurs* (2000), "it takes guts to lose money;" it also takes discipline to see beyond the short-term through to success. Guts alone are not enough. The individual entrepreneur needs guts and discipline. In battle bravery is only part of the requirement for a soldier, sailor, and airman/woman. In their analysis of the 1982 conflict between the UK and Argentina over the Falkland Islands (Malvinas), Max Hastings and Simon Jenkins comment that, although individual Argentinians were brave, as a conscript army they often lacked the discipline that characterized the British assault forces of 3 Commando Brigade and 5 Infantry Brigade, composed as they were of Royal Marines, elements of the Parachute Regiment, Gurkhas, and Guards Regiments and supporting units. In the end, although outnumbered nearly three to one, and at the end of a very long 8000-mile supply line with air cover limited to a handful of naval Sea Harriers, it was discipline that won the conflict and forced an Argentinian surrender.

As quoted earlier, Tom Bower claims that Sir Richard Branson, despite being the UK's best known entrepreneur, has a "butterfly mind" that flits from project to project. In his analysis of Branson's problems with British Airways however, Martyn Gregory paints a picture of a man who was capable of considerable disciplined focus on the problem and crucially a man who knew when to call in experts to assist him. In the previous section the need to know one's limitations was discussed and part of the entrepreneurial discipline is to know when help is needed and who to go to. Seeking assistance is not a sign of weakness but one of strength and discipline. It is those who do not seek help until it is too late, whether from over-confidence or fear of losing face, who tend to fail.

We all have a degree of discipline – we have to in order to survive in a society that lays down rules. This discipline can be worked on to make us more disciplined. To some it is more natural than others but with effort it is available to all who want it.

Hopefully you see how a picture is being built up:

VISION → SELF-BELIEF → DISCIPLINE

Entrepreneurship is not one single attribute or skill; it is a mosaic of a number of them combining to assist in reaching the vision.

Time management

As time management requires discipline it is considered here under attributes. You may feel that it is purely a skill and should be in the skills section. Where it is placed is less important than that it is considered.

Ken Bogas' (the first case study in the next chapter) mother believes that her son thinks that each day contains 25 hours and he never has enough time. That is not unusual for an entrepreneur; there are never, or so it seems, enough hours in the day. With practice, however, even the busiest person can reclaim some time by delegation or dealing with time bandits. Too many entrepreneurs let their health and their family suffer due to a time famine – they don't seem to have enough time for themselves, their families and the business, and it is the business that eats up all the time. To paraphrase the Bible, what will it profit an entrepreneur if they become exceedingly wealthy but lose their family and their life to a stress-related disease?

Time bandits are those things that steal time from the individual. Meetings that needn't be attended; inspections that somebody else could do; reports that could be read in summary form – the list is endless. The solution? Identify them and fight them. Ask: do I have to do this? Is this important, is it urgent, are important and urgent the same? – the answer is: no they are not!

Time decay

As Peterson points out in *The Complete Entrepreneur*, when one was young there always seemed to be plenty of time. As one grows older the realization that time is limited and the time left to do anything is actually decaying becomes a more and more important factor in planning. Unlike a government that has a fixed term of office, humans have no idea for how long they will be on this earth and thus not only is time decaying but we actually have no idea by how much it is doing so. It is therefore very important that time is managed as effectively as possible.

Delegation

Delegation is a useful method of aiding time management and one that appears very difficult for the entrepreneurial individual to do.

Delegation is not just asking or telling somebody to do something. In delegation you also have to give them a portion of your power and authority plus the resources to carry out the task, it is the "loan" of power that the entrepreneurial individual finds difficult. The person to whom you delegate is able to act with your authority and, whilst they are then responsible for the task, the accountability for it being carried out properly – i.e. who carries the can? – remains with you. Responsibility can be delegated, accountability cannot.

Those who realize that delegating and giving away a little of their power can have a wonderful payback in freeing up time are the lucky ones. Too many entrepreneurs and managers are too afraid to let go of power and thus try to do everything themselves, making the time famine even more acute.

Risk-taking

It might be thought that risk-taking is a negative attribute. However, in the case of the entrepreneurial individual it is the taking of calculated risks after a careful analysis of the factors involved and an assessment of the chances of success that is important. Without risk-takers there would be no progress – somebody has to take the first step.

In discussing entrepreneurism it must not be thought that risk in these terms means a lack of caution. Entrepreneurial individuals weigh risks very carefully and then after a careful analysis of all the internal and external factors may take a risk that a more conservative-minded individual would eschew, but only if the pay-off is high and the risk is not likely to endanger the vision or their financial survival. Risk is very much a relative term.

In the *ExpressExec* material *Creating the Entrepreneurial Organization*, the case of Sir Richard Branson is used when considering risk. It might be thought that starting an international airline in the highly competitive market of the mid-1980s when few of the world's airlines were profitable was a risky undertaking. Add to that the fact that the main competitor would be one of the few profitable airlines at the time – British Airways (BA) – and this makes the venture seem even more of a gamble, especially when the organization (and its leader) concerned had no experience whatsoever in the industry – only a vision of a new style of airline with the Virgin brand. However, Richard (later Sir Richard) Branson and Virgin initially chartered just a single Boeing 747 for one year only and, as he states in his autobiography, *Losing My Virginity* (1998), the most the organization would lose would be £2mn (about $3.2mn) per year – a small amount to the Virgin Group as a whole. Despite the competition from BA (some of which has been deemed unfair and has been described by Martyn Gregory in his book *Dirty Tricks* as a secret war against Virgin Atlantic), Virgin as an air carrier has been very successful and has expanded its route network into Asia and Southern Africa. Each development has been a risk but a carefully calculated and affordable one. Sir Richard Branson forms the subject of one of the case studies in the next chapter.

Analyzing the risk

The entrepreneurial individual will soon acquire the skills of analysis to be covered later. Banks and venture capitalists will want to know that the risks have been considered and that contingency plans exist for worst case scenarios. Entrepreneurial individuals are not foolhardy, they are, to use an old English word, "canny" – a mixture of worldly-wise and shrewd. Their actions may look risky but they are thought through risks that are worth taking.

Blame

However hard the individual tries, things will always go wrong. As projects grow, the entrepreneurial individual will be employing staff to carry out an increasing number of functions. How are they treated when something goes wrong?

First, the entrepreneurial individual must take the blame for their own mistakes and not try to shift it onto somebody else. It is easy to accept applause when things go well, less easy to take the brickbats when the opposite occurs, but if it is your fault, admit it and learn. Face is not lost but respect will be gained. Too many politicians lose public respect not because they make mistakes but because they never seem to admit them.

It is almost impossible for an organization to be entrepreneurial if its members are watching their backs all the time. People have to be allowed to make genuine mistakes provided that they learn from them. It is often said that far more is learnt from things that go wrong than things that go right!

This does not mean that those who do not learn or those who exceed their authority should not be censured – they should. However, honest mistakes that aid organizational learning and development can be tolerated, as they may be the foundation of future progress. It is worth reflecting that the person who never made a mistake never made anything!

Concern for the customer

It should be self-evident that no customers equals no business. Unfortunately it is only too easy to find large and small organizations that do not appear to have realized that this is, in fact, the first law of business.

When one examines organizations that seem to pay no regard to their customers it transpires that the customers have often been in what Jones and Strasser in *Why Satisfied Customers Defect* referred to as hostage situations. If you are on vacation and there is only one gas station in a small town and your petrol gauge is near empty then that is where you will make a purchase – you are in fact a hostage to that organization. Since the end of World War II, as communications technology has shrunk the world and markets have become more global, customers are less content with a hostage state of affairs. Modern organizations, even very small local ones, must compete for custom. Gaining and, crucially, retaining customers requires a knowledge of the needs and wants of the customer, what Peters and Waterman in *In Search of Excellence* referred to as "closeness to the customer."

Even complaints, properly handled and with the situation recovered, can assist this process as complaints can tell an owner or manager who is prepared to listen and take action a great deal about their organization.

The ability to relate to customers is a key attribute for any entrepreneurial individual. However demanding they may be they are the source of revenue and success – no entrepreneur can do without them.

Whatever the reality, it is important that the entrepreneurial individual appears honest and trustworthy and a person people will want to do business with. Personality is as important as business skills. Most entrepreneurs have a keenly defined aura of charisma. Be an exciting person to be with. Be knowledgeable about the world and make every customer feel as if they are the most important person in your world.

Creativity

The final attribute is creativity. The individual entrepreneur has to see the possibilities and devise strategies for achieving them. Pushing the envelope has to become second nature to them.

For every possible course of action consider alternatives. What could be done if . . .? Remember that people once said that the world was flat, that railway trains moving at 60mph (about 95km/h) would suffocate their passengers, that iron ships would sink, etc. Inventors and entrepreneurs challenge assumptions, the former technically and the latter in bringing ideas to the market-place.

Thinking is as important to the entrepreneurial individual as doing because it allows the vision to be clarified into actions. Entrepreneurs, being at the cutting edge of whatever business they work in, have to be creative. In many cases they are rewriting or even breaking the rules. Christopher Price has said, "Business rules are good: break them." Perhaps this should be changed to: business rules are necessary so re-write them to fit the changed circumstances. To do that one needs to be creative.

THE SKILLS NEEDED BY THE ENTREPRENEURIAL INDIVIDUAL

It is worth noting that there is no particular occupational skill in the list that follows – it is not a necessity, as will be discussed later.

Analysis

The entrepreneurial individual who succeeds does so because they know what is going on in the world. They are able to acquire information either personally or through others, analyze it and then use it to move towards their vision.

The SPECTACLES analysis

The SPECTACLES analysis has grown out of the traditional PEST (Political, Economic, Social, Technological) analysis. This author considered that additional components have become necessary to cope with an increasingly more complex business and social environment and published the concept of the SPECTACLES analysis in *Mastering the Business Environment* (2001).

The individual components of the analysis impact not only upon the organization or project of the entrepreneur; they also impact upon each other in a complementary manner. There are more details about the SPECTACLES analysis in *Creating the Entrepreneurial Organization* – companion material to this in the *ExpressExec* series.

The SPECTACLES acronym stands for: Social, Political, Economic, Cultural, Technological, Aesthetic, Customer, Legal, Environmental, and Sectoral. It is these areas of the external environment that the entrepreneur needs to examine for their impact on his or her plans. From them will be generated a set of threats and opportunities that can be acted upon.

Analysis is a skill that requires discipline (see above). Any business analysis needs to be carried out in a logical, planned way. Part of the analytical discipline is not rejecting information that does not seem to fit in with the entrepreneurial individual's plans – such information is often the most important as it may point to deviations and variations.

Successful business activities also require careful analysis of the internal aspects of the individual entrepreneur's organization including finance and his or her own personality – a crucial factor when considering individual entrepreneurship.

Networking

Individual entrepreneurs tend to know a great number of people. The ability to network is crucial to their success.

Successful entrepreneurs ensure that their contact lists are up to date and accessible. They always have the telephone number or e-mail address to hand. The arranging of such information is a skill that can be developed. Entrepreneurs research guest lists before events (even of the social kind) so that they can be briefed as to the likes, dislikes, and business interests of the people they are likely to meet.

The Internet can provide considerable assistance to the entrepreneurial individual as it has considerably eased the process of business communication through e-mail and even video-conferencing.

Networking skills also include communications, conversational, and vocabulary skills. The individual will want to build up a relationship as fast as possible (see later) and access information in the most efficient manner. They also need to put across their own charisma as expeditiously as possible.

The more the individual entrepreneur is aware of themselves, the more they can network with others and gain the synergy that can be developed from a combination of efforts.

Building relationships

Linked to networking (above) is the importance of relationships. By studying motivation and other aspects of human psychology the entrepreneurial individual is in a better position to influence those who they will need to assist them in making their vision a reality.

Nobody, however good or entrepreneurial, is able to bring a project to fruition without the assistance of others and thus good working relationships are all-important. It can be so easy for the entrepreneurial individual to become immersed in their own ideas that they forget to communicate to those working with them what is happening and why, and this can quickly lead to a breakdown in relationships and lessen the effort that others put in towards the vision.

Negotiation

The process we undertake to get somebody to do something (without using physical coercion) is known as negotiation. There are many texts on negotiation and the all-important art of compromise. The better the networking and the stronger the relationships, the easier negotiations usually are. Compromise is nearly always required and a key negotiating skill that the entrepreneurial individual must develop is that of knowing precisely how much they can afford to give when compromising and assessing quickly and accurately the bottom line of the other partner in the negotiation.

Most negotiations are carried out in a ritual manner as illustrated in Fig. 6.1 (with the entrepreneur indicated by "entrep." and the other side in the negotiation by A).

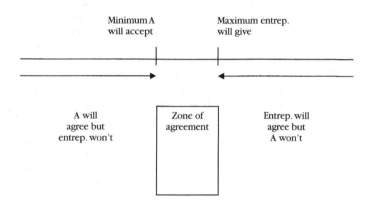

Fig. 6.1 Negotiation – zone of agreement.

Provided that the minimum A will accept is lower than the maximum the entrepreneur can offer, agreement is possible. If not then there is no zone of agreement and it is unlikely that there will be a transaction (Fig. 6.2).

Once a negotiation has broken down it can be very difficult to restart the process, as both sides tend to retreat to their original or even more extreme positions. It is important therefore to ensure that maximum information and flexibility is on hand in order to enter the zone of agreement as soon as possible if there is to be a good chance of agreement.

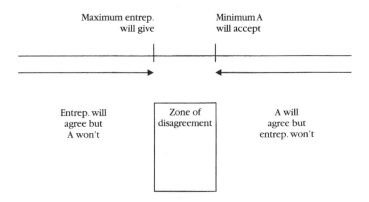

Fig. 6.2 Negotiation – zone of diagreement.

Selling

Selling is, in essence, a form of negotiation with similar concepts as those above being used. There are two things, however, that the entrepreneurial individual must sell long before there is a product or service to offer to customers.

The first of these is the vision and the second is the entrepreneur themselves. It is a characteristic of individual entrepreneurship that the entrepreneur may be as important a factor in making a deal as the nuts and bolts of what is on offer. It has been claimed of Branson (see next chapter) that he is a self-publicist as if this is somehow a fault. If you are, or aspire to be, an entrepreneurial individual then you need to be packaged, promoted, and sold in a manner that will gain you maximum coverage. There is absolutely nothing wrong with seeking publicity (provided the means and the actions are legal) – it is, after all, nothing more than personal advertising.

It is not unusual for the more successful entrepreneurial individuals to employ their own publicists. Even if you have not reached that stage, the media can still be used for stories that link you and what you are offering. Victor Kiam, who died in 2001, and was the owner of Remington, gained global fame when he featured in his own "I liked the shaver so much that I bought the company" advertisement.

That particular advertisement not only sold a shaver but also Kiam as a trustworthy, "nice" individual.

Finance

No business can survive without the resource we call money. Whilst the entrepreneurial individual does not need to be an accountant (there are plenty of accountants around whose services can be bought-in), they do need to understand the financial concepts that are used in business.

There are plenty of books and college programs that can provide assistance in this respect. As, hopefully, more and more money comes in it will assist the entrepreneur if they can keep a rough track of it themselves. The courts are often asked to rule on cases where creative individuals believe they have been cheated by their financial advisors. A little knowledge on the entrepreneur's part might help nip any such activities in the bud.

Sources of finance

The entrepreneurial individual also needs to know where finance and assistance can be acquired. Banks and venture capitalists are useful sources. Governments often provide tax breaks and free advice to those starting or expanding business operations. This is where the networking skills can be put to excellent effect – find out who will put money in and what help the government or other organizations can provide.

The role of occupational skills

It is not always necessary for the entrepreneurial individual to possess any particular occupational skills. Branson knew nothing about the airline business before setting up Virgin Atlantic. In high-tech industries such as computer-related sectors it may be necessary to understand programming, etc. – it all depends on the area of operation.

Some knowledge may be required for credibility but often those closely associated with an occupation may be too close to its traditions to see new possibilities.

If an entrepreneurial individual has an idea, they can always buy-in the relevant professional expertise as Branson did when he recruited a highly experienced staff from other air-carriers to manage the Virgin Atlantic operation.

Support and health

Entrepreneurship can be hard work and stressful and thus it is important to keep as healthy as possible. Stress can be reduced by exercise (see *Stress Management* in the *ExpressExec* series) and this will also help keep the body healthy.

Discipline not only applies to work practices; it can be just as important in respect of food and drink (especially alcohol and stimulants). A healthy body aids a healthy mind, as the old saying goes!

It is also important that the entrepreneurial individual has the support of their nearest and dearest. As the vision can consume much of an entrepreneur's time it is vital that space and time is made available for family relationships – they are just as important as, if not more important than, business ones.

Do not neglect those who care about you. If all goes well you will want to share the success with them. If it goes wrong, you will need them more than ever.

KEY LEARNING POINTS

» Attributes and skills can and should be developed.
» Analysis of the external and internal environments is very important in entrepreneurial activities.
» Missing skills and occupational competence can always be bought-in.
» The health aspects of the entrepreneur should not be neglected.
» Time management is a vital skill and discipline for the entrepreneurial individual.
» Delegation involves giving away a portion of power but can free up a great deal of time.
» Responsibility can be delegated, accountability cannot.
» Time must be made for family relationships.

In Practice:

Entrepreneurial

Individual Success

Stories

» Ken Bogas – Vancouver, Canada
» Sir Richard Branson – UK
» Kwek Leng Beng – Singapore

There are many, many successful entrepreneurial individuals. In choosing examples for this chapter, the author has tried to balance those who have become global names and those who are just at the start of their entrepreneurial activities. The case study on imageData in Chapter 4 could just as easily have been in this chapter as Steve and Tina Medin are good examples of local entrepreneurs whose business is growing.

KEN BOGAS – VANCOUVER, CANADA

Despite the façade still being under construction, as soon as it opened over 100 customers began to eat at Coco Pazzo in Kerrisdale, Vancouver each evening.

The local press thought that it might be the Hernando's Hideaway syndrome, the thrill of making that unexpected discovery, but most likely, they commented, the restaurant's immediate popularity was due to the fact that people were curious about what chef/owner Ken Bogas had been up to since he parted business company with his brother-in-law Umberto upon the sale of their former Vancouver restaurant, Mangiamo. Vancouver residents have become used to Bogas getting an enterprise up and running and then moving on to his next project – typical entrepreneurial behavior.

Ken Bogas has been in the catering business since he was 15, over 26 years ago. Working first for others, he has learnt his trade and developed a love of, and a skill for, preparing Italian cuisine. Coco Pazzo is his fourth business venture and continues the success he has achieved as a small-scale entrepreneur.

His first entrepreneurial enterprise was the Café Europe in Vancouver, which he started in 1982, followed by Saltimbuca in 1992. By this time Bogas had become well-known for his flamboyant style coupled with good food and an interesting ambience to his operations.

Bogas instituted a major conceptual change at his restaurant, Mangiamo, opened in 1994. The restaurant became very popular with both business people and with local sports stars, the latter also attracting fans and followers – a form of free endorsement and excellent advertising. Whereas in other similar establishments there has always been a clear divide between the food preparation areas and the customers, not so at Mangiamo. Normally, the more exclusive and expensive the establishment, the more what happens behind the scenes is hidden.

One of the great charms of the New York diners and the UK fish and chip shops is that you can often see your food being prepared and even talk to the staff preparing it. By introducing the radical change of removing the partitions between customers and the kitchens and even providing a bar for customers to sit and eat at that is directly linked to the kitchen area, Bogas allowed his growing number of customers to interact with the staff directly.

Whilst a risky change, he saw this close link between customers, staff, and the product as a key factor in the success of the establishment which received very good reviews in the Canadian press, and the customers seem to love it. The opening up of hitherto forbidden areas gave customers a new respect for the kitchen staff and provided an opportunity for all of the staff, and not just the waiters and bus boys as in more traditional restaurant arrangements, to relate to the customers. This required the recruitment of staff who could deal with the change to direct contact with customers. With the kitchen opened up, errors could be seen more easily. Bogas demonstrated one of the great tenets of quality – if the operation is transparent, the customer can see exactly what is going on and thus quality standards need to be the highest possible. Equally, Bogas' customers, because they were involved, became very loyal. By virtue of the layout of Mangiamo they were more than a mere customer and the staff more than just employees. Bogas' changes made everybody a part of the organization.

For his new Coco Pazzo operation, Bogas converted a former bank into a neighborhood-style Italian restaurant. Much of the physical work was provided by the 42-year-old Bogas himself.

It had been months of difficult work but his efforts were successful in that he not only created another visually appealing and workable space, as was Mangiamo, but one that also manages to be both cozy and spacious at the same time, in line with Bogas' personality. The design elements include the rustic familiarity of tile, brick, wood, ironwork, faded tapestry, and terracotta and marigold coloring that are reminiscent of Italy (even though Bogas' mother qualifies for a UK passport in addition to her Canadian one and his father is of Greek origin), but there is also a set of easy chairs in front of a fireplace, a wine cellar in a former bank vault, and a small garden patio under development. The tables are large and sturdy, not the usual telephone tables for two, and the attractive, well-lit bar is immense – a definite attraction for the diner who is eating alone or is in a hurry.

In true Bogas style, the kitchen at Coco Pazzo is an open one so the customers can watch him as he does his "whirling dervish cooking style thing," as newspaper reviews have described it. Bogas' cooking is about entertainment as well as cuisine, although, like Sir Richard Branson whose career is examined next, the once wild guy now seems calmer and more mature.

Bogas certainly works very long hours and the hard work has paid off.

Ken Bogas may be an entrepreneur in a small way but each venture builds on the last and he has a loyal clientele. What Bogas has done, anybody can. The step of moving away divisions between the kitchen and the eating area could have failed. If it had, Bogas could have re-erected the partitions but his belief was that it would work and he has been proved correct. His operation may not be in the same league as Microsoft or Virgin but that makes him no less of an entrepreneurial individual. He is dedicated to success, quality, and doing things differently – the marks of an entrepreneurial individual.

Ken Bogas – time-line

(See Fig. 7.1 on page 63.)

KEN BOGAS – KEY INSIGHTS

» Dedication and hard work.
» Prepared to take chances, as in opening up kitchen spaces.
» Reputation for high quality tinged with a degree of eccentricity.
» Considerable emphasis on customer care – repeat business is very important.
» Takes pleasure and pride in what he does.

SIR RICHARD BRANSON – UK

Sir Richard Branson is an exceptionally well-known personality and businessman in the UK and across the globe. It may be that Branson is

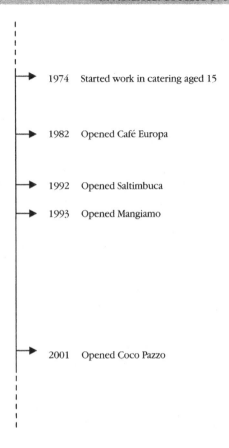

Fig. 7.1   Time-line: Ken Bogas.

interested in money. In June 2001, *Forbes Global Magazine* reported his wealth at $1.3bn. Somebody who has that much money has no apparent need to work and yet Branson appears as active as ever. As an outstanding entrepreneur he must be motivated by something other than hard cash.

His business ventures have included record producing, publishing of both books and music, soft drinks, contraceptives (condoms), financial services, rail transport, energy, mobile telephones, Internet services (an ISP – Virgin Net), his airline, Virgin Atlantic, and two failed attempts to run the UK National Lottery – all using the Virgin brand. He is also well-known for a record-breaking crossing of the Atlantic in a large, fast speedboat, and his ballooning exploits across the Atlantic and the Pacific.

Branson, made Sir Richard in 2000, is also probably unique in the world in that he has not only been quoted as the UK business personality most admired by the nation's young but also as the person UK parents would most like their children to emulate.

To many the names Branson and Virgin are synonymous and this could present a problem. Virgin as a group of organizations presents a classic "spider's web" power/club culture as depicted by Charles Handy (*Gods of Management* [1978]) whereby all the power and energy lies very much at the center, i.e. in Branson's hands. No Branson could mean no Virgin, very much in the manner of the problems of ITT (International Telephone and Telegraph) from 1979 when the charismatic CEO, Harold S. Geneen, retired and his carefully assembled empire began to unravel, as described by Richard Tanner and Anthony G. Athos (1981).

For all the praise lavished on Branson in the UK and elsewhere this does not mean that he is a candidate for sainthood or that all his ventures have been successful. Virgin Cola has not presented the challenge to Coca-Cola and Pepsi Cola that Branson prophesied and Virgin Trains (albeit operating on routes urgently in need of track renewal and new signaling) produced some of the worst post-privatization punctuality statistics in the UK. To understand Branson and his position within the UK you are advised to consult three texts, full details of which are contained in Chapter 9. The first, *Losing My Virginity*, is his autobiography, the second, *Dirty Tricks* by Martyn Gregory, is a pro-Virgin examination of the problems Virgin Atlantic encountered with British Airways, and the third, *Branson* by Tom Bower, takes a highly critical look at Branson and his activities.

Branson began his entrepreneurial activities whilst still a schoolboy, with his first step into proper business in 1968 with the launch of

Student magazine for which he elicited advertising copy and revenue without revealing that he was still in his teens.

In 1970 the young Branson saw an opportunity for mail order record sales. His original operation had an illegal facet to it in that some records were sold free of UK tax, being really intended for overseas sales. The extent of this customs evasion is a matter of conjecture but that it happened is a matter of fact. A year later in 1971 he opened his first record shop (in London) and in 1972 he bought a manor house in Oxfordshire (some 50 miles [about 80km] or so to the North of London) to use as a recording studio, launching the Virgin record label and a music publishing business in 1973.

In 1973 Virgin Records released Mike Oldfield's best-selling album, *Tubular Bells*, and the cash generated provided the organization and Branson with the necessary financial stability to expand and also with a reputation in the music business that attracted other top artistes and bands. The controversial punk group The Sex Pistols signed up with the label in 1977, followed by Phil Collins in 1981 and Boy George and Culture Club in 1982.

Branson had already opened his first nightclub in 1978, and Virgin Vision (later Virgin Communications) and Virgin Games in 1983.

All of these developments in Branson's entrepreneurial career had one thing in common: they were aimed at the youth culture sector of the market. Virgin was a brand that appealed to youth. The brand name was, according to Branson, chosen because he and his associates were "complete virgins at business."

Branson had long admired the UK entrepreneur Freddie Laker whose Skytrain airline operation offering cut-price flights from the UK to the US had been placed into bankruptcy in 1982. Laker had claimed that a consortium of international airlines had driven him out of business by unfair practices, and after years of legal wrangling in the US (where President Reagan took the unprecedented step of dismissing a Grand Jury in order, it is believed, to secure UK support for arms limitation talks with the then USSR – the UK government wanted the legal action stopped as it would delay the privatization of British Airways (BA), one of the main defendants), Laker received at least a degree of cash compensation.

In 1983 a US lawyer named Randolph Fields approached Branson with the concept of an airline operating from London's second airport (Gatwick, where Laker had been based) to New York using the landing and take-off slots left vacant by Laker Airways. Branson was taken with the idea. He already knew from Laker that just appealing to the young would not work for an airline. Laker had only offered business class travel late on in Laker Airways' existence and it is from such premium traffic that much of the revenue for an airline is gained.

Despite advice from friends that this was not a good business area to enter, Branson found that he could lease a single Boeing 747 and that the total cost for one year's operation would be around £2mn ($3.2mn), money that he could well afford given the success of the music side of the business.

The idea of a Branson-run airline with flight attendants in bright red uniforms and Branson often on board dressed, as always, in his pullover (sweater) and sporting his "cheeky" grin (he eventually came to be ridiculed in BA as the "grinning pullover") proved a winner and the airline, Virgin Atlantic, was soon able to expand.

Unfortunately for Branson the expansion of his airline proved none too popular at the headquarters of the recently privatized BA. Branson was soon accusing BA of operating a "dirty tricks" campaign to cast doubt on the financial stability of Virgin Atlantic. This unfortunate episode has rumbled on for some time with the issues before both the US and the UK courts. At one stage Branson claimed that BA had libeled him personally and BA counter-sued that it was their organization that had been libeled. UK courts had not been known for huge awards of damages in libel cases so it was an historic moment in 1993 when the case was settled with Branson receiving a record sum of £610,000 (about $976,000) plus all the legal costs (which were huge) from BA.

The "dirty tricks" issue has been the subject of Martyn Gregory's book and a UK television documentary, and Branson and Virgin received considerable support from the public. There is no doubt that the culture of Virgin Atlantic as regards publicity and marketing is very different to that of BA. Branson did not endear himself to the then BA chairman, Lord King of Wartnaby, or the then CEO, Sir Colin Marshall, when in July 1991 he leapt out of a truck at the entrance to Heathrow Airport and, dressed in a pirate costume complete with stuffed parrot, slipped a Virgin logo over the tail of the scale model of a BA *Concorde* that stands at the convergence of the main airport access roads. Branson was celebrating Virgin finally being granted landing and take-off rights at Heathrow, rights that had been bitterly opposed by BA.

In fairness to King and Marshall they took a highly bureaucratic and customer-unfriendly nationalized airline to become a model for customer service and efficiency in just a few short years. Branson's complaint was not that they were successful but that they used their near monopoly position in the UK to discourage any competition.

Virgin Atlantic now flies not only to the US but also to the Far East and South Africa.

By 1988 Virgin Atlantic was a regular winner of airline awards and had become the UK's number two international carrier. Paradoxically when the domestic/European carrier, British Midland, applied to operate transatlantic flights, it was BA and Virgin who opposed the move that would have provided extra competition to both themselves and United & American who also operated from Heathrow to the US. Nevertheless, in 2001 British Midland joined the transatlantic air carriers club. Competition can make for very strange bedfellows indeed!

In 1985, as an adjunct to the airline business Virgin Holidays commenced operations, and in 1986 the Virgin Group, but excluding the airline, club, and holiday operations, was floated on the London Stock Exchange. The excluded areas were brought together as the Voyager Group.

It was in 1987 that Branson began to expand his international operations with the establishment of Virgin Records' operations in the US and Japan. Further deals with Japanese interest were to follow, including an investment partnership with the Fujisanki Communications Group in 1989 and a 50-50 joint venture with Marui to open and operate a chain of megastores in Japan in 1990.

Branson is quite clearly a man with considerable self-belief (see Chapter 6) and a need for control. When Virgin went public, some of that control passed to shareholders, especially those representing institutional interests. Thus in 1998, Branson announced a management buyout of the Virgin Group following the 1987 stock market crash. This allowed him to buy back the shares at a reasonable price.

In 1992 Branson took one of the hardest decisions of his life so far when he sold his "baby," Virgin Music, to Thorn EMI. At the time Virgin Atlantic was in the midst of the "dirty tricks" issue with BA and the money gained from the sale, over $1bn, gave him the cushion to fight the airline's battles. Nevertheless, it was clearly a difficult decision as Virgin Music had been the foundation from which all the other businesses had been built. Branson himself says that he wept after the sale but then realized how stupid a newspaper headline that read "Man gains $1bn and then weeps" would appear.

By 1994 there was a myriad of Virgin businesses operating in a variety of sectors including radio and television. The UK's first national commercial rock radio station was Virgin FM, and Virgin Megastores had signed a partnership agreement with the US video rental giant, Blockbuster.

Perhaps the first real mistake came in the same year with the launch of Virgin Cola, a product to challenge the dominance of Coca-Cola and Pepsi Cola. Tom Bower has pointed out that, despite considerable marketing, sales in 1995 were only 3.1% of the global market according to a *Nielsen* report. Coca-Cola and Pepsi Cola are very much entrenched in the global market-place and displacing them would be a mammoth task.

Equally the award of the franchise to run the UK rail networks for cross-country services in 1996, and the important West Coast Mainline between London and Edinburgh via Crewe and Preston in 1997, has seen Virgin move into difficult territory. These were not cutting edge operations. They comprised routes that were amongst the earliest railways in the world, dating from the early Victorian period. The physical layout of the track makes high-speed running such as achieved by the French TGV difficult. Virgin Trains did not have the best punctuality record between the start of operations and 2000, with large numbers of customer complaints and unfavorable comments from the rail regulator who oversees the franchised operations. In their defense it must be said that Virgin had already ordered new stock of the latest design to be introduced from 2001 onwards and to replace the outdated equipment inherited from the nationalized British Rail. Nevertheless, Virgin's (and thus Branson's) image was not enhanced by the sight of delayed trains struggling into London's

Euston Station. In 1998, Virgin Rail acquired the Perth (Scotland) based global transportation group Stagecoach as a partner, with Stagecoach holding 49% of the company and Virgin 51%. This synergy between Stagecoach's excellence in land transportation and Virgin marketing, etc., may well prove to be the solution for Virgin Rail.

In 1993–4 Branson made a bid to run the first ever UK National Lottery as a non-profit operation. The eventual winner of the bidding was Camelot who continued to operate the lottery until a re-bidding process in 2000. The two contenders for the re-bidding were Camelot and Branson's "People's Lottery." First nobody won, then Branson was given another month to amend the financial package and finally Camelot appealed to the High Court and were reinstated as the lottery operators. It is clear from his comments that Branson was very annoyed at this turn of events. A number of those involved from the National Lottery Commissioners' side resigned but Branson had still failed a second time to win the lottery franchise.

Branson exemplifies most of the skills and attributes of the entre-preneurial individual considered in Chapter 6. Whilst somewhat uncon-ventional, the risks he takes are calculated, as shown by Virgin Atlantic. He has incredible self-belief in his abilities and considerable charisma. Whilst Branson had no expertise in the airline industry, he assembled a highly professional team to run Virgin Atlantic with himself being the public face.

Branson has also showed that he is very adept at networking. Photographs of Branson and public figures often appear in the press. Even UK royalty in the person of the late Princess Diana appeared to give her blessing to his enterprises. Princess Diana named the first of Virgin Atlantic's Airbus Industrie aircraft and another aircraft was named *Spirit of Sir Freddie* after Sir Freddie Laker who, as covered above, Branson admired greatly. It was Sir Freddie who told Branson that his mistake had been not to take court action against BA and other airlines when he believed that they were acting against Laker's interests. His advice to Branson was to "sue the ********", which Branson did.

Princess Diana was much loved both in the UK and across the world, as witnessed by the public show of grief after her untimely death in a traffic accident. For Branson to have her as part of the image was a considerable networking coup, as was her note congratulating him when BA paid the libel damages.

Branson has also showed that he has financial skills in the manner in which money from an established enterprise is used to support the newer initiatives.

He can also sell himself, as witnessed by the publicity gained from his high profile ballooning exploits around the world. When a balloon with Virgin on the envelope and Branson as a crew member makes the television news, that is excellent advertising (unless, of course, it were to involve a tragedy).

In his critical 2000 account of Branson, Tom Bower wonders whether the financial problems he alludes to, the failed lottery bids, the failure of Virgin Cola, etc., and the poor customer satisfaction position of Virgin Trains, means that the "Branson Bubble," as he calls it, has burst.

Time alone will tell, but it would be a brave man or woman (or maybe a foolish one) who would bet that, even if Bower is right, Branson would not make a comeback given his personality and his obvious entrepreneurial skills. Could an entrepreneur like Branson be kept down? – the writer of this material doubts it very much.

Sir Richard Branson – time-line

(See Fig. 7.2.)

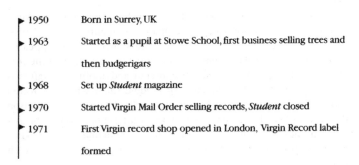

1950	Born in Surrey, UK
1963	Started as a pupil at Stowe School, first business selling trees and then budgerigars
1968	Set up *Student* magazine
1970	Started Virgin Mail Order selling records, *Student* closed
1971	First Virgin record shop opened in London, Virgin Record label formed

Fig. 7.2 Time-line: Sir Richard Branson.

1972	Recording studio opened
1978	First night club opened. One off charter of aircraft due to delay in Caribbean leads to first Virgin flight
1979	Loss of £900,000 recorded for Virgin Group
1982	Boy George and Culture Club sign up with Virgin Records. Profit for year is £2m
1983	Virgin Vision, Virgin Games and Vanson Developments formed
1984	Profit £11m. Virgin Atlantic and Virgin Cargo formed. First attempt at Atlantic Blue Riband
1985	Virgin Holidays formed
1986	Part of Virgin Group floated on the London Stock Exchange raising £30m. Successful Blue Riband attempt
1987	Virgin Records launched in US and Japan. Atlantic Balloon crossing attempted. Branson and Lindstrand rescued in Irish Sea. British Airways take over British Caledonian leading to complaint by Virgin Atlantic to the UK Monopolies and Mergers Commission
1988	67 of the 102 UK record shops sold to W H Smith for £23m. 10% of Virgin Atlantic sold to Japanese interests for 36m and 25% of Virgin Music to Japanese interests for £100m
1990	Trans-Pacific balloon flight abandoned

Fig. 7.2 (*continued*).

1991	Virgin publishing formed. Virgin Atlantic receives permission to operate flights UK to Japan. Complaints by Virgin against British Airways alleging dirty tricks. Virgin granted landing and take-off rights at London Heathrow instead of London Gatwick
1992	Virgin Music sold to Thorn EMI for £560m
1993	British Airways settles libel case with Branson and Virgin Atlantic. Branson bids to operate UK lottery but is unsuccessful
1994	Virgin Cola launched. Virgin Atlantic begin UK to Hong Kong service
1995	Virgin Financial Services formed
1996	Virgin net formed as ISP (Internet service provider). Virgin Rail awarded its first UK rail franchise following privatization of UK rail network
1997	Virgin Rail awarded the Glasgow to London via the UK west coast rail franchise
1998	49% of Virgin Rail bought by Stagecoach, Virgin hold 51%
2000	Branson receives knighthood
2000	Unsuccessful 2nd bid for UK lottery

Fig. 7.2 (*continued*).

SIR RICHARD BRANSON – KEY INSIGHTS

» Self-belief: Branson has a very confident public persona.
» Never misses out on a chance for publicity.
» Started with a sector he knew, i.e. the young and music, and then moved on.
» When starting Virgin Atlantic he knew little about airlines so he recruited a first-class team around him.
» Appears committed to quality and customer service.
» Was prepared to sell his "baby" – Virgin Music – when money was needed. There is little room for sentimentality in business.
» Appears trustworthy.
» Was prepared to buy back the organization and take it back into private ownership when necessary.
» Was prepared to defend himself when necessary, e.g. the court cases against BA.
» Has excellent networking skills
» Appeals to a wide sector of society.

KWEK LENG BENG – SINGAPORE

The third case study of entrepreneurial individuals involves not just a singleton but a family. Families of entrepreneurs are rarer in the West than in Asia, where family relationships are given greater prominence in business matters.

Singapore is an independent city-state republic in south-east Asia, comprising one major island and more than 50 smaller adjacent islets, located off the southern tip of the Malay Peninsula. Singapore Island, the one major island, is separated from Malaysia on the north by the narrow Johor Strait, over which passes the famous causeway linking the city to the mainland. To the south, it is separated from the Riau Archipelago of Indonesia by Singapore Strait, an important shipping channel linking the Indian Ocean to the west with the South China Sea on the east. It is this proximity to a major shipping lane that has led to the prosperity of Singapore and its high numbers of entrepreneurs pro rata when compared to other regions of a similar size. The city of Singapore at the south-eastern end of the island is one of the most important port cities and commercial centers of south-east Asia.

With a population of over three million, Singapore is densely populated. The population is ethnically diverse and consists of Chinese (78%), Malays (14%), Indians (7%), and Other (1%). The country has four official languages – English, Mandarin Chinese, Malay, and Tamil, with English as the administrative language.

Industry has grown rapidly since the 1960s, and Singapore now produces a diversity of goods, including chemicals, pharmaceuticals, electronic items, clothing, plastics, rubber products, steel pipes, plywood, and processed foods. Shipbuilding and petroleum refining are also important.

Singapore is a major world port and has extensive dock facilities along Keppel Harbour on the southern coast. Much of its trade involves the trans-shipment of goods produced in the region. In the late 1980s annual imports cost $40.3bn, while exports earned $38bn. Singapore's principal trading partners include the US, Japan, Malaysia, China, Taiwan, Germany, and Hong Kong. Singapore is also a member of the Association of South-East Asian Nations (ASEAN). Tourism and international banking are important sources of foreign exchange revenue. The country has one of the largest international airports in Asia, and a 26km rail line that crosses Johor Strait and links with the Malaysian railroad system.

Singapore has been a trading center almost since the recording of history began, lying as it does in such a strategic position.

The modern city was founded in 1819 on the site of a fishing village by the British colonial administrator Sir Thomas Stamford Raffles (after whom Singapore's famous Raffles hotel is named) and deeded to the British East India Company in 1824 by the Sultan of Johor. In 1826 Singapore was incorporated into the UK, of the Straits Settlements colony. Singapore's advantageous location on the narrow passage between the Indian Ocean and the South China Sea turned Singapore into a major commercial center. After World War I Britain designated the island its principal naval base in East Asia and undertook extensive military construction. During World War II Singapore was captured and occupied by the Japanese until 1945.

In 1946 Singapore was made a separate Crown colony and on June 3, 1959, it became a self-governing state in the Commonwealth of

Nations. On September 16, 1963, Singapore, Malaya, North Borneo, and Sarawak united to form Malaysia but in 1965 Singapore was separated from Malaysia and became a sovereign state, remaining in the Commonwealth and becoming a member of the United Nations. In December of that year the island was proclaimed a republic.

This brief history of Singapore has been included because it is the republic's geographic status and its cultural diversity as a result of its history that has made it a nourishing area for entrepreneurship.

The Chinese influence is very strong in Singapore, as shown by the population figures above. Kwek Leng Beng's father, Kwek Hong Png, arrived in Singapore from mainland China in 1928. The eldest of four brothers, he worked in a small shop belonging to a relative, saving up his money until in 1941 he was able to start a small trading company. Unfortunately, on December 8 (the 7th in Hawaii, being on the other side of the date-line), the Japanese attacked the UK, US, and Dutch military and commercial centers in the Pacific and Indian Ocean areas and within a few short weeks Singapore was occupied and the Chinese population subjected to considerable brutality.

Fortunately for the family all four brothers survived the war and were thus able to take part in the huge growth of Asian commerce that began with post-war reconstruction and the granting of independence from the various European colonial powers, mainly the UK, France, and the Netherlands.

The company, the Hong Leong Group, is named after Kwek Hong Png's youngest brother and in the 1960s it moved to set up operations within Malaysia itself, both the Malayan and Singaporean operations diversifying into property. Real estate in Singapore is precious and thus property is a hot commodity.

Kwek Hong Png died in 1994, having retired a decade earlier after handing over the overall direction of business to his eldest son Kwek Leng Beng (hereafter referred to as Kwek). The Hong Leong Group is the largest conglomerate in Singapore, and real estate operation, of which Kwek holds the majority share, is over twice the size in terms of capitalization as its nearest rivals.

Kwek expanded the Group's operations into hotels – a not unusual development for companies with an interest in real estate. By 2000 Kwek owned 115 hotels spread across the globe. The brands included

Copthorne, the Plaza in New York, and the Gloucester and Britannia in London, together with other hotels in Asia.

Kwek and his brothers have also retained close links with their home base in Singapore, in Malaysia, one brother being President of the Singapore Chinese Chamber of Commerce and Industry.

Other Hong Leong Group activities include banking, construction and building materials, semi-conductors, and a desire to work with higher education to improve educational opportunities in the region.

If any family showed how self-belief and hard work can build up a business empire, going from nothing in 1928 to owning 300 companies with an annual turnover of $2.5bn by 2000, it is Kwek and his brothers and father. By working together they have shown how the family can be a very tight and useful business network. In many ways they have kept close to their core business of trading and then real estate. The move into hotels is a rational one for a real estate based organization as hotels are very much influenced by real estate prices. Hotels are also a useful way to achieve a global presence because of the way hotel chains are organized to provide a linkage of accommodation for customers moving between centers.

Kwek Leng Beng – time-line

(See Fig. 7.3 on page 77.)

KWEK LENG BENG – KEY INSIGHTS

» The use of the family as an entrepreneurial network.
» Setting up in a region amenable to entrepreneurial activities and on a major trade route.
» Entrepreneurs can recover even from wars.
» Moving outwards in geographic small steps, Singapore to Malaya in the first instance.
» Choosing a suitable vehicle (in this case hotels) for global expansion.

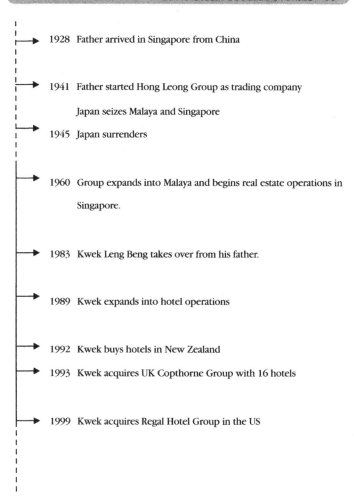

1928 Father arrived in Singapore from China

1941 Father started Hong Leong Group as trading company

       Japan seizes Malaya and Singapore

1945 Japan surrenders

1960 Group expands into Malaya and begins real estate operations in
       Singapore.

1983 Kwek Leng Beng takes over from his father.

1989 Kwek expands into hotel operations

1992 Kwek buys hotels in New Zealand

1993 Kwek acquires UK Copthorne Group with 16 hotels

1999 Kwek acquires Regal Hotel Group in the US

Fig. 7.3 Time-line: Kwek Leng Beng.

Key Concepts and Thinkers in Individual Entrepreneurship

A GLOSSARY FOR THE ENTREPRENEURIAL INDIVIDUAL

Allowable weakness – see Chapter 10. The negative side of a positive strength. If the weakness is corrected there is a danger that the strength will be diluted. In the same way as a coin cannot have just one side, allowable weaknesses are connected to the strength and must be managed not eliminated.

Butterfly mind – often used in connection with creative or entrepreneurial people, a butterfly-minded person moves on from project to project leaving others to carry out further development, implementation, and routine tasks.

Chunking – the splitting up of tasks or objectives to make them more manageable and less prone to failure.

Culture – the values, attitudes, and beliefs ascribed to and accepted by a group, nation, or organization. In effect, "the way we do things around here."

Delegation – a process where a subordinate is asked to carry out a task that you are accountable for, having been provided with a portion of your power and authority plus the necessary resources. Responsibility to do something can be delegated but you retain the accountability for it being carried out and in the correct manner, etc.

Entrepreneur – a business person who is constantly seeking new opportunities and is prepared to take a calculated risk in order to move their business forward.

Entrepreneurial attributes – the attributes most commonly associated with the entrepreneurial individual are:

» vision
» commitment
» self-belief
» discipline
» risk-taking
» concern for the customer
» creativity.

Entrepreneurial skills – the skills the entrepreneurial individual needs to develop are:

» analysis
» networking
» building relationships
» negotiation
» selling
» finance.

Exchange rates – the value of one currency against another. As oil is often priced in $US, all those in business have a vested interest in the rate of exchange between the $US and their home currency; indeed between their currency and the currency of any of their suppliers, customers, or competitors.

Internet-related products – a fertile area for many recent entrepreneurs, Internet-related products are those that are used in association with the World Wide Web. They can be computer software products such as search engines or portals, Internet service provision (ISPs), or new ways of selling and marketing, e.g. Amazon.com, with book and music sales.

ISP (Internet Service Provider) – these companies provide the link between Internet users and the World Wide Web, usually by subscription to their services. AOL (America On Line) is a well-known example.

Negotiation – the process whereby two or more parties try to find common ground (a zone of agreement) so that a transaction of some kind may occur on terms that they can all accept.

Networking – the business relationships that the individual builds and develops in order to facilitate progress.

Routines – tasks that need to be undertaken regularly and which are concerned with the maintenance of organizational operations or customer relationships.

Search engines – the method and software used by Internet users to search for pages on the World Wide Web. Web pages are registered with the search engine databases. Yahoo!, Lycos, Excite, etc. are commonly-employed search engines. They are nearly always funded by advertising and are thus free to the user.

SPECTACLES analysis – an analysis that considers the Social, Political, Economic, Cultural, Technological, Aesthetic, Customer, Legal, and Sectoral external factors that provide opportunities and threats to the organization. Entrepreneurial organizations monitor these factors regularly in order to be in a position to grasp an opportunity as soon as possible.

Time bandits – those activities that steal time from people. They include unnecessary activities and those that could be carried out by somebody else (see delegation above).

Time decay – the process whereby less and less time is available as a project or even a life progresses. As the life span of humans is not fixed, time decay is difficult to quantify.

Time famine – attempting to do too much in too short a time leads to a time famine where there is not enough time to do anything well. Delegation of tasks can ease this problem.

URL (Uniform Resource Locator) – the unique address for a Web page.

USP (Unique Selling Point) – introduced in Chapter 10 as part of the 10 steps to success, a USP is that unique feature that makes the organization's products or services different from those of its competitors.

KEY THINKERS

All of the books referred to in this section are listed fully in Chapter 9.

Covey, Stephen R.

Personal attributes are very important to the success of the entrepreneurial individual. The US writer Stephen R. Covey has become known for his work on the habits of effective people. He believes that lives should be organized around natural forces rather than trying to manage limited time (see time decay above and in Chapter 6) around manufactured priorities.

Covey is important in a consideration of entrepreneurial individuals because he considers issues such as potential and the innate human need for progress. He believes that life and work should be principle-centered.

His original work on the *Seven Habits of Highly Effective People* has been developed to consider families and leadership, again on a principle-centered basis. In *First Things First*, Covey examines the importance of effective time management.

Whilst individuals might not agree with all of Covey's ideas, they are challenging and challenge is precisely what the entrepreneurial individual thrives on.

There are also Covey leadership centers around the world dedicated to passing on his ideas and many of his books are also available on audio tapes.

Stephen Covey has written a large number of books, the most relevant from the point of individual entrepreneurship are listed below.

Highlights

Books:

» *Principle-Centered Leadership* (1990).
» *First Things First* (1994).
» *The Seven Habits of Highly Effective People* (1994).
» *The Seven Habits of Highly Effective Families* (1998).

Drucker, Peter F.

Born in Vienna in 1909, Peter Drucker has been a major force in managerial and organizational thinking since publishing his first ideas in 1939.

Drucker has shown a lifelong appreciation of the creative possibilities of business. His ideas helped shape the dramatic expansion of American industry in the post-World War II period and influenced worldwide thinking about business.

Drucker believes that, although it is not so very difficult to predict the future, it is actually pointless. Many futurologists make quite accurate predictions. They do a good job of foretelling some but not always the most important things. To Drucker, far more important are the fundamental changes that happened though no one predicted them or could possibly have predicted them – these are often the events that the entrepreneurial individual is able to use to his or her advantage. He believes that organizations and individuals cannot make decisions for the future. Decisions are commitments to action and actions are always in the present. However, actions in the present are also the one and only way to make the future. Managers are paid to take effective action and they can do so only in contemplation of the present, and by exploiting the changes that have already happened. To enable today's manager to be ahead of this different tomorrow, indeed to make it *their* tomorrow, is the aim of Drucker in *Managing in Times of Great Change* (1995).

Drucker may not always be the easiest to read but he is one of the most challenging, and both the entrepreneurial individual and the organizations that they form will thrive on the challenges that Drucker presents, given his vast experience stretching back over many years.

Drucker's autobiography, *Adventures of a Bystander*, (he has been anything but!) reflects on his life and those he has met.

In 1985 Drucker turned his attention to entrepreneurship in his book *Innovation and Entrepreneurship*, in which he argues for the imposition of discipline in entrepreneurship and innovation in a similar manner to the structured way the Japanese rebuilt their commercial operations post-1945. Discipline is sometimes one of the hardest things an entrepreneur has to achieve and yet, as Drucker argues, many wonderful ideas need not only creativity, vision, drive, and commitment, but also discipline if they are to reach the market-place and be successful.

There is also the Drucker School of Management and the Peter F. Drucker Foundation for Non-profit Management, both in the US, the latter concentrating on management functions within public sector (national and local government, military, etc.) operations.

Drucker has produced over 29 separate books and a myriad of articles, etc. The most useful from the standpoint of the entrepreneurial organization are listed below.

Highlights

Books:

» *The Practice of Management* (1955).
» *Managing for Results* (1964).
» *Innovation and Entrepreneurship* (1985).
» *Managing for Turbulent Times* (1993).
» *The Executive in Action – Managing for Results, Innovation and Entrepreneurship* (1996).

» *Adventures of a Bystander* (1998).
» *Management Challenges for the 21st Century* (1999).

Farrell, Larry C.

Farrell has written to explain how the power of entrepreneurship can be harnessed by individuals, organizations and entire countries to compete and thrive in the twenty-first century. He sees the twenty-first century as the entrepreneurial age and believes that the twentieth was the managerial age. Examining four fundamental practices of the world's great entrepreneurs, he attempts (successfully) to provide simple strategies for creating and implementing business plans on all levels, from the mission statement to day-to-day organization practices. Farrell offers advice not only to individual entrepreneurs, but also explains how entrepreneurial culture can be developed and fostered in corporate and governmental settings, hence his importance to this material. In organizational terms he shows how decision-makers can facilitate high-speed innovation, set free the potential and often hidden genius of the average worker, translate job satisfaction into high-quality production, and cultivate customer satisfaction and loyalty.

Immensely readable, Farrell makes the point that anybody or any organization can be entrepreneurial, as it is not so much a "thing" as a way of thinking.

Highlights

Books:

» *The Entrepreneurial Age* (2001).

Heinecke, William E.

Working with journalist Jonathon Marsh, William E. Heinecke, the CEO of The Minor Group in Thailand, has produced a guide of 21 Golden Rules for the entrepreneurial global business manager.

Whilst one can sometimes be suspicious of books that seem to offer a shortcut to success, by allying his considerable successful entrepreneurial ability to the skills of his journalist colleague, Heinecke has produced a very useful framework for the entrepreneurial organization to use as it grows and develops.

His 21 Golden Rules may sound a little trite when viewed in isolation but together they provide a powerful and robust structure for an organization to use. They are as follows.

1 Find a vacuum and fill it. (It is worth remembering that a vacuum can be huge or a small niche – fill it and there is no room for anybody else!)
2 Do your homework.
3 You won't be committed if you're not having fun. (The fun side of work is often forgotten and even derided but it can be a crucial motivator.)
4 Work hard, play hard.
5 Work with other people's brains.
6 Set goals (but go easy on vision). Note – goals should always be C-SMART (Customer-centered, Specific, Measurable, Agreed, Realistic, and Timely (Cartwright, *Mastering Customer Relations* (2000)). Comments about goals, vision, and Heinecke are contained in Chapter 6.
7 Trust your intuition.
8 Reach for the sky (at least once).
9 Learn to sell.
10 Become a leader.
11 Recognize a failure and move on.
12 Make the most of lucky breaks.
13 Embrace change as a way of life.
14 Develop your contacts.
15 Use your time wisely.
16 Measure for measure. (Use benchmarking and understand your performance and quality standards.)
17 Don't put up with mediocrity.
18 Chase quality not cash.
19 Act quickly in a crisis.
20 After a fall, get back in the saddle quickly.
21 Be content.

Highlights

Books:

» *The Entrepreneur* (2000).

Jones, John W.

Working in Illinois, Jones has produced a useful work on time management and its links with the overall management function. His ideas will be of considerable use to the creative and entrepreneurial and are presented in an easy-to-read style. Jones is concerned with what he calls "high-speed management" as required by modern industries and especially customers.

He offers particular insights into the management of information and decision-making within tight time-frames, issues that often beset the entrepreneurial individual.

Latterly, Jones has considered the implications of the Internet and e-commerce in *Virtual Entrepreneurs – Electronic Commerce in the 21st Century*.

Highlights
Books:

» *High Speed Management* (1993).
» *Virtual Entrepreneurs – Electronic Commerce in the 21st Century* (1999).

Peters, Tom

From the publication of *In Search of Excellence* (in 1982) onwards, Tom Peters has become one of the best-known names in the fields of management, change, quality, and entrepreneurship. Indeed in his first bestseller – *In Search of Excellence*, written with Bob Waterman – autonomy and entrepreneurship were seen as one of the key attributes of the excellent organization. His message has been delivered on a global basis and has reached a huge audience, initially of senior, but more recently including junior, staff.

Three quotes express the importance of the effect Tom Peters has had on modern organizational thinking:

» "In no small part, what American corporations have become is what Peters has encouraged them to be." – *The New Yorker*;
» "Peters is ... the father of the post-modern corporation." – *Los Angeles Times*;
» "We live in a Tom Peters world." – *Fortune Magazine*.

Tom Peters describes himself as a prince of disorder, champion of bold failures, maestro of zest, professional loudmouth, corporate cheerleader, and a lover of markets. *Fortune Magazine* has also referred to him as the "Ur-guru" (guru of gurus) of management and compares him to Ralph Waldo Emerson, Henry David Thoreau, and Walt Whitman. *The Economist* has titled him the "Uber-guru" (literally "over-guru"). His unconventional views led *Business Week* to describe him as "business' best friend and worst nightmare." Best friend because of the challenges he throws out which, if taken up, can lead to success, and worst nightmare because his ideas have challenged conventional thinking – always an uncomfortable thing to do. It is these challenges that make Peters compelling and necessary reading for the entrepreneurial individual.

Peters followed up on the success of *In Search of Excellence* with four more best-selling hardback books: *A Passion for Excellence* (1985, with Nancy Austin); *Thriving on Chaos* (1987); *Liberation Management* (1992) – acclaimed as the "Management Book of the Decade" for the '90s; *The Circle of Innovation: You Can't Shrink Your Way to Greatness* (1997); and a pair of best-selling paperback originals: *The Tom Peters Seminar: Crazy Times Call for Crazy Organizations* (1993); and *The Pursuit of WOW!: Every Person's Guide to Topsy-Turvy Times* (1994). The first of Peters' series of books on *Re-inventing Work* were released in September 1999: *The Brand You 50*, *The Project 50* (as an e-book, it knocked Stephen King out of first place on the e-bestsellers list!), and *The Professional Service Firm 50*.

Peters also presents about 100 major seminars globally each year. Organizations and increasingly individuals pay considerable sums for their staff to attend these seminars. He has also authored a large number of articles for various newspapers and popular and academic journals, including: *Business Week*, *The Economist*, *The Financial Times*, *The Wall Street Journal*, *The New York Times*, *Inc.*, *Fast Company*, *The Washington Monthly*, *California Management Review*, *The Academy of Management Review*, *Forbes*, and *The Harvard Business Review*.

Peters' philosophy for the reinvention of business and organizations is about change, giving power to people, and encouraging entrepreneurship. He recognizes that we are in a changing, sometimes chaotic, world and sees that as an opportunity not a threat for organizations with the courage to move forward – ideal subjects to interest the entrepreneurial individual. The research for *In Search of Excellence* was under the auspices of the McKinley organization and was a review of excellent companies in the US and how America could re-establish its position in world trade. From those early ideas and the attributes contained within (see Chapter 6) has developed the Peters philosophy, a philosophy very much concerned with entrepreneurship.

Highlights
Books:

» *In Search of Excellence* (1982) (with Waterman, R.).
» *A Passion for Excellence* (1985) (with Austin, N.).
» *Thriving on Chaos* (1989).
» *Liberation Management* (1992).
» *The Pursuit of WOW!* (1994).
» *The Circle of Innovation* (1997).
» *The Brand You 50* (1999).
» *The Project 50* (1999).
» *The Professional Service Firm 50* (1999).

Peterson, Mark A.
Whilst one might have a cynical approach to anybody who offers to sell you "the complete anything," Mark Peterson's *The Complete Entrepreneur* is a useful reference guide for the entrepreneurial individual to keep on their bookshelf.

Peterson has arranged the book in a series of sections, none of them detailed but containing enough material to trigger further investigation. Although written for the US reader and thus using US business and financial terms, the book should be easily understood by other English speakers.

The sections Peterson covers are many and are worth listing as they act as an aide-memoire for the prospective entrepreneur:

» basic requirements for entrepreneurs;
» basic concepts about building wealth;
» assessing and taking reasonable risk;
» false starts and their inevitability;

- » opportunity;
- » partners;
- » banks;
- » buying into existing businesses;
- » customers;
- » employees;
- » running a business;
- » time management;
- » investments;
- » information technology;
- » blame;
- » experts;
- » contracts and the law; and
- » selling or retiring.

Highlights

Books:

- » *The Complete Entrepreneur* (1996).

Price, Christopher

Until March 2000, Price was the information technology correspondent of the London *Financial Times*, having worked for the newspaper for 10 years. His first book, *The Internet Entrepreneurs*, was published in 2000 and profiles a number of well-known (e.g., Jeff Bezos of Amazon.com) and also lesser-known names who have shown their entrepreneurial skills in Internet-related activities.

He also edits a financial services Website.

Highlights

Books:

- » *The Internet Entrepreneurs* (2000).

Other Authorities

A number of texts have been produced by and/or about some of the more prominent entrepreneurs and the organizations they have been involved with. Full references for a number of these are provided in Chapter 9.

Many of these texts focus on the personality of the individual and thus are of particular interest to the user of this material.

A small selection of useful texts to read include the following.

» About Amazon.com and its founder Jeff Bezos:
  » *Amazon.com*, Spector, R.
» About The Body Shop and its founder Anita Roddick:
  » *Business as Usual*, Roddick, A.
» About Microsoft and Bill Gates:
  » *Gates*, Manes, S. & Andrews, P.
» About Sony and its founder Morita:
  » *Made in Japan*, Morita, A.
» About Virgin and Richard Branson:
  » *Losing My Virginity*, Branson, R.;
  » *Branson*, Bower, T.;
  » *Richard Branson – the Authorised Biography*, Brown, M.; and
  » *Virgin King*, Jackson, T.

Resources for the Entrepreneurial Individual

- » Books
- » Magazines and journals
- » Trade and professional journals
- » College and university programs
- » Websites

BOOKS

Note: Dates of books in this chapter may differ from those shown in previous chapters. The dates here are of editions that have been revised from the date of first publication as shown in the chapter material.

Adair, J. (1990), *Understanding Motivation*. London, Kogan Page.

Adair, J. (1997), *Effective Communication*. London, Pan.

Belbin, M.R. (1981), *Management Teams – Why They Succeed or Fail*. Oxford, Heinemann.

Belbin, M.R. (1993), *Team Roles at Work*. Oxford, Butterworth Heinemann.

Belbin, M.R. (1996), *The Coming Shape of Organization*. Oxford, Butterworth Heinemann.

Bower, T. (2000), *Branson*. London, 4th Estate.

Branson, R. (1998), *Losing My Virginity*. London, Virgin Publishing.

Brown, M. (1992), *Richard Branson*. London, Headline.

Brown, P. (1996), *Anita Roddick and The Body Shop*. London, Exley.

Bryan, L., Fraser, J., Oppenheim, J., & Rall, W. (1999), *Race for the World*. Boston (MA), Harvard Business School Press.

Cartwright, R. (2000), *Mastering Customer Relations*. Basingstoke, Palgrave (Macmillan).

Cartwright, R. (2001), *Mastering the Business Environment*. Basingstoke, Palgrave (Macmillan).

Covey, S.R. (1994), *First Things First*. New York, Simon & Schuster.

Covey, S.R. (1990), *Principle-Centered Leadership*. New York, Simon & Schuster.

Covey, S.R. (1998), *The Seven Habits of Highly Effective Families*. New York, Simon & Schuster.

Covey, S.R. (1994), *The Seven Habits of Highly Effective People*. New York, Simon & Schuster.

Dearlove, D. (2001), *Business the Richard Branson Way*. Oxford, Capstone.

Drucker, P.F. (1985), *Innovation and Entrepreneurship*. Oxford, Butterworth Heinemann.

Drucker, P.F. (1999), *Adventures of a Bystander*. London, John Wiley.

Eddy, P., Potter, E., & Page, B. (1976), *Destination Disaster*. London, Hart-Davis.

Farrell, L.C. (2001), *The Entrepreneurial Age*. Oxford, Windsor.

Foot, D.K. & Stoffman, D. (1996), *Boom, Bust, and Echo*. Toronto, Macfarlane, Walter & Ross.

Gregory, M. (1994), *Dirty Tricks - British Airways' Secret War Against Virgin Atlantic*. London, Little, Brown & Co.

Handy, C. (1978), *Gods of Management*. London, Souvenir Press.

Harris, P.R. & Moran, R.T. (2000), *Managing Cultural Differences*. Houston, Gulf Publishing Co.

Hastings, M. & Jenkins, S. (1983), *The Battle for the Falklands*. London, Michael Joseph.

Heinecke, W.E. & Marsh, J. (2000), *The Entrepreneur-21 Golden Rules for the Global Business Manager*. Singapore, John Wiley & Sons (Asia).

Herzberg, F. (1960), *Work and the Nature of Man*. New York, World Publishing.

Jackson, T. (1984), *Virgin King*. London, HarperCollins.

Jones, T.O. & Strasser, W.E., Jnr, (1995), *Why Satisfied Customers Defect*. Harvard Business Review, Nov.-Dec. 1995, pp. 88-99.

Jones, J.W. (1993), *High Speed Management*. San Francisco, Jossey Bass.

Jones, J.W. (1999), *Virtual Entrepreneurs - Electronic Commerce in the 21st Century*. Rosemont, BPRI.

Marquardt, M.J. & Berger, N.O. (2000), *Global Leaders for the 21st Century*. Albany, State University of New York Press.

Morita, A. (1986), *Made in Japan*. New York, HarperCollins.

Pascale, R. & Athos, A. (1981), *The Art of Japanese Management*. New York, Simon & Schuster.

Peters, T. & Waterman, R. (1982), *In Search of Excellence*. New York, Harper & Row.

Peterson, M.A. (1996), *The Complete Entrepreneur*. New York, Barron's Educational.

Porterfield, J.D. (1993), *Dining by Rail - The History and Recipes of America's Golden Age of Railroad Cuisine*. New York, St. Martin's Press.

Price, C. (2000), *The Internet Entrepreneurs*. Harlow, Pearson.

Roddick, A. (2000), *Business as Usual*. London, HarperCollins.

Saunders, R. (2000), *Amazon.com*. Oxford, Capstone.

Trompenaars, F. (1993), *Riding the Waves of Culture*. London, Economist Books.

For information about the EU and the Social Charter
Pettinger, R. (1998), *The European Social Charter - A Manager's Guide*. London, Kogan Page.

For information on the Internet
Aldrich, D.F. (1999), *Mastering the Digital Marketplace*. New York, John Wiley.
Kennedy, A.J. (1999) *The Internet - The Rough Guide 2000*. New York/London, Rough Guides.

For information about Microsoft and Bill Gates
Manes, S. & Andrews, P. (1994), *Gates*. New York, Simon & Schuster.
Dearlove, D. (2001), *Doing Business the Bill Gates Way*. Oxford, Capstone.

For information on Nokia
Merriden, T. (2000), *Cold Calling - Business the Nokia Way*. Oxford, Capstone.

For information on J.P. Morgan and the Titanic
Davie, M. 1986, *Titanic - The Full Story of a Tragedy*. London, Bodley Head.
Gardiner, R. & Van der Vat, D. (1995), *The Riddle of the Titanic*. London, Weidenfeld & Nicolson.

MAGAZINES AND JOURNALS

All broadsheet type newspapers, *Washington Post*, *New York Times*, *Herald Tribune*, London *Times*, *Daily Telegraph*, *Observer*, *Le Monde*, etc., provide useful analysis of news and financial/business matters. The more individual entrepreneurs know, the easier it is for them to see opportunities. The entrepreneurial individual should ensure that they read at least one of the quality newspapers from their country each day as well as listening to and watching current affairs and relevant programs on the radio or television.

The following, most of which are published on-line as well as in hard copy (see Websites at the end of this chapter), are useful sources of information about markets, competitors and developments. The Websites should be accessed for subscription rates, samples, and special subscription offers.

Business 2.0

Business and financial daily carrying articles, etc., of use to individual entrepreneurs. The importance of scanning such material for items of possible interest cannot be overstated.

The Economist

Weekly current affairs magazine with a global approach. *The Economist* carries general current affairs news in addition to analysis and market news on a global basis. Issued both as a print version and on-line. Available by subscription or from news-stands.

Financial Times

UK daily carrying financial reports and analysis. Available on subscription or from news-stands.

Forbes

Forbes is a leading company providing resources for the world's business and investment leaders, providing them with commentary, analysis, relevant tools, and real-time original reporting on business, technology, investing, and lifestyle.

The weekly *Forbes* magazine is also available on-line and whilst mainly designed for a US audience is read on a global basis.

Forbes often carries articles and commentaries on entrepreneurs and entrepreneurial activities.

Other linked products from *Forbes* include the following.

» *Forbes Global*, covering the rise of capitalism around the world for international business leaders. Contains sections on Companies & Industry, Capital Markets & Investing, Entrepreneurs, Technology and *Forbes Global Life*.

» *Forbes Newsletters*, including the following.

  » *Forbes Aggressive Growth Investor*, a monthly newsletter recommending the 50 best growth and momentum stocks to own now as determined by a proprietary multi-dimensional computer analysis of over 3000 stocks.

  » *Gilder Technology Report*, covering the smartest, most profitable way to invest in technology. Buy tomorrow's biggest technology winners today when their shares are cheap and you can potentially multiply your wealth 10 to 100 times. The *Gilder Technology Report* will show you how.

  » *Special Situation Survey*, with monthly stock recommendations, hold or sell advice on each recommendation, and special investment reports.

  » *New Economy Watch*, a newsletter that looks at Internet-based companies.

Harvard Business Review

The leading business and management resource. Read worldwide and features contributions by the leading names in business and management. Published 10 times a year and available by subscription. Linked to the world-renowned Harvard Business School.

Management Today

Published by the Institute of Management in the UK, available monthly to members or by subscription. Often contains useful articles on issues concerned with entrepreneurship, together with a regular feature on the subject. For example, the June 2001 issue contains information about the young UK entrepreneur Reuben Singh, whilst the May 2001 issue contains an interview with the man who made Amstrad a leading name in UK consumer electronics – Alan Sugar. These profiles are a useful and informative way for the entrepreneurial individual to gain an idea of the attributes and skills of those who are a little further ahead in their journey.

TIME

TIME Magazine, whilst originally a US product, has a global readership and is one of the most important current affairs and commentary magazines in existence. To appear on the cover of *TIME* is to have made it; to be the *TIME* man/woman of the year is a considerable honor indeed.

TIME covers a huge range of issues and is thus useful to the entrepreneurial organization as a source of material for the SPECTACLES/SWOT analyses covered in Chapter 5.

The print version is available either on subscription or from newsstands.

TIME was the first news magazine to publish on-line, beginning in 1993, and launched TIME.com in 1994. According to *Nielsen NetRatings*, TIME.com is the most trafficked news magazine site on-line. TIME.com draws over five million visits per month and receives over 32 million monthly page views. The site covers the events impacting the world each day and offers its own perspective on the latest news. There are also sections entitled: Nation, Education, World, and Health.

LIFEmag.com looks at the defining moments and great events of our lives through photography. The site features a Picture of the Day, This Day in *LIFE*, and a searchable magazine and cover collection dating back to 1936.

ONmagazine.com is the on-line complement to *ON*, the million-plus monthly personal-tech magazine from the editors of *TIME*. The site is a before-you-buy authority on new gadgets and Web services. ONmagazine.com features a new hands-on review every weekday, along with jargon-free how-to-buy guides for popular product categories.

Wall Street Journal

US financial daily carrying analysis, financial, and other commercial news, plus company results. Available on subscription or from newsstands.

TRADE AND PROFESSIONAL JOURNALS

Each entrepreneurial individual will be operating in a particular market-place with a set of products, services, or ideas unique to the entrepreneur to at least some extent.

In addition to understanding the general world of business and commerce there will be specific sectoral requirements and knowledge that the individual needs to acquire.

Nearly every occupation, profession and business sector has journals and magazines dedicated to it.

These journals and magazines are one of the most valuable sources of information available to the entrepreneurial individual. They are often the first place that new developments, products, and ideas are unveiled and they often contain key information on the major players in that particular area.

In addition to the written word there are trade and professional associations across the globe dealing with nearly every type of business activity. Membership may well be worthwhile but it is worth remembering that such organizations exist to exchange information – there will be a requirement to give as well as to take.

COLLEGE AND UNIVERSITY PROGRAMS

It has become fashionable for colleges and universities to set up faculties, departments, and programs concerned with innovation and entrepreneurship. Some of these offerings are very expensive and have developed from conventional MBA (Master of Business Administration) programs. Whilst they might provide some of the skills required for entrepreneurship, it is a fact that many entrepreneurs have done very well with no formal business or management qualifications at all. Entrepreneurship is not management. Sir Richard Branson has no management qualifications – when he needs a manager he hires a good one.

It is important to be especially aware of educational establishments that are less well-known and yet still offer programs in entrepreneurship. Check out their track record in the field and the record of those they are employing to teach and facilitate – if they are successful entrepreneurs then all well and good, but if not, what are they doing teaching the subject?

WEBSITES

www.business2.com	Business 2 Website
www.cocopazzo.bc.ca	Coco Pazzo/Ken Bogas Website
www.easyJet.com	easyJet Website
www.economist.com	*Economist* Website

www.forbes.com	*Forbes* Website
www.ft.com	*Financial Times* Website
www.hbsp.harvard.edu/ products/hbr	*Harvard Business Review* Website
www.imagedata.com	imageData Website
www.inst-mgt.org.uk	Institute of Management Website
www.lycos.com	Lycos Website
www.microsoft.com	Microsoft Website
www.nokia.com	Nokia Website
www.time.com	*TIME Magazine* Website
www.tompeters.com	Tom Peters Website
www.VermontTeddyBear	Vermont Teddy Bear Website
www.virgin.com	Virgin Website
www.wsj.com	*Wall Street Journal* Website
www.yahoo.com	Yahoo! Website

Ten Steps to Assist the Entrepreneurial Individual

The 10 steps:

1 look for a product, service, idea, etc. that is different to that being carried out by others;
2 having found a product, service, idea, etc., take steps to acquire the resources to implement it;
3 know the external environment;
4 know yourself and your vision;
5 acquire skills, develop attributes;
6 consider the risks and don't be afraid of failure;
7 set objectives;
8 communicate the vision;
9 ensure support; and
10 build up a network

are a starting point for the entrepreneurial individual.

There is also the question of luck. It has been said of people like Bill Gates of Microsoft or Sir Richard Branson that they are lucky. Are they, or is it that they have made sure that they are in the right place at the right time? Much of what some call luck is actually the result of a careful analysis of the world and then placing oneself where things are happening.

Even to win a lottery you have to buy a ticket, i.e. you have to take an action that will put you in contention. Perhaps luck is winning the lottery when you haven't bought a ticket!

Entrepreneurial individuals do not rely on luck – they make things happen.

The entrepreneurial individual needs to adapt each of the steps below to their own particular circumstances. Every business situation is unique and thus step 1 is vital in order to understand the specific environment within which the individual intends to operate. This makes the analytical skills required by the entrepreneurial individual all the more important because, whilst others may be able to assist, at the end of the day it is the individual's personal analysis of which they are an integral part that may make the difference between success and failure.

1. LOOK FOR A PRODUCT, SERVICE, IDEA, ETC., THAT IS DIFFERENT TO THAT BEING CARRIED OUT BY OTHERS

Entrepreneurs move things forward. They will not wish to enter a field and be like everybody else. They will want to:

» do the same but deliver it in a different way;
» do something new but deliver it in an established way; or
» do something new and deliver it in a different way.

The first two are often safer as at least one of the variables remains within everybody's so-called comfort zone, i.e. they are familiar with that way of working.

Amazon.com sells books, an activity that is hundreds of years old, but in a new way, over the Internet. Ken Bogas had new ideas for how to run a restaurant, but implemented them within a traditional set up (but with some walls removed), whereas everything that imageData did with Websites was brand new at the time and used the PC, a new means of delivery.

Difference becomes a USP (Unique Selling Point) and that is what customers respond to, as the entrepreneurial individual and their organization will have something that the customer can identify it with.

2. HAVING FOUND A PRODUCT, SERVICE, IDEA, ETC., TAKE STEPS TO ACQUIRE THE RESOURCES TO IMPLEMENT IT

Many people have ideas, few actually take the necessary steps to implement them – they are the entrepreneurial individuals. There may be many things that need to be done to facilitate implementation including:

» seeking partners;
» seeking finance;
» registering patents;
» appointing agents and dealers;
» setting up manufacturing;
» arranging logistics; and
» marketing.

The list will differ from project to project and it is important that the individual spends time ensuring that they have thought of as many as possible. The implementation of some of the above can then be delegated (see later) as they are routine and not entrepreneurial activities.

3. KNOW THE EXTERNAL ENVIRONMENT

The importance of analysis has already been stressed throughout this material. The individual entrepreneur needs to consider a whole range of external factors before embarking on a development as it is a consideration of these factors that will provide an indication of the potential opportunities and threats.

A SPECTACLES analysis – standing for Social, Political, Economic, Cultural, Technological, Aesthetic, Customers, Legal, Environmental, Sectoral – will allow a wide range of factors to be taken into account.

4. KNOW YOURSELF AND YOUR VISION

In addition to analyzing the external environment the entrepreneurial individual needs to consider their strengths and weaknesses in order to build on the former and take steps to see that the latter do not inhibit their entrepreneurial activities. Weaknesses are less of a problem if they are known. Some of the entrepreneur's weaknesses will be what are known as allowable weaknesses, i.e. the opposite side of a positive strength. Lose the weakness and the strength may go as well. Creative people can have weaknesses in communicating. Force them to concentrate on the communication and their creative output may drop. Weaknesses can often be overcome by bringing in somebody who can complement your strengths as an employee or partner - see step 9.

In formulating the vision ensure that it is manageable and translated into a format that can be communicated to others - see step 8.

5. ACQUIRE SKILLS, DEVELOP ATTRIBUTES

It is unlikely that you will have all the skills and attributes fully developed at the start of an entrepreneurial career. Consider what skills are needed and acquire them. There are a number of sources available:

» books and journals - see Chapter 9;
» training courses and college/university programs, but remember the caution in Chapter 9; and
» colleagues and peers.

Never be afraid to ask others who have been successful, many of them may be only too willing to help.

Beware of "get rich quick" schemes and programs that promise you that "you too can be a successful entrepreneur." It takes hard work and time to build up the necessary skills base. There is no quick solution.

6. CONSIDER THE RISKS AND DON'T BE AFRAID OF FAILURE

Risks should be carefully analyzed. If a failure as a result of taking a risk will not jeopardize the survival of the enterprise, it may well be worth taking. Remember how Branson took the risk of running his airline for the first year - he could afford to lose that much money.

Failures are something to be learnt from. We learn far more from things that go wrong than we ever do from things that go right. Many psychologists believe that a certain degree of failure is necessary for motivation and challenge. If it goes right all the time we can become as dispirited as if it always goes wrong. Columbus was a failure - he was supposed to be finding a new route to India - but there are still statues to him all over the world!

If a person really cannot stand failure then he or she can never be a true entrepreneur. In the famous poem by Rudyard Kipling entitled *If* and introduced in Chapter 6, the second verse reads:

"If you can dream – and not make dreams your master;
If you can think – and not make thoughts your aim;
If you can meet with Triumph and Disaster
And treat those two impostors just the same;
If you can bear to hear the truth you've spoken
Twisted by knaves to make a trap for fools,
Or watch the things you gave your life to, broken,
And stoop and build 'em up with worn-out tools;"

Every budding entrepreneurial individual should read that poem and follow its advice. Risk and failure need to be put into perspective. Risk nothing, gain nothing.

7. SET OBJECTIVES

Every vision needs steps to see its realization. The successful entrepreneur sets objectives that are C-SMART – Customer-centered, Specific, Measurable, Agreed (others will be involved in fulfilling objectives and their agreement and buying-in to them is vital), Realistic (remember – what may be realistic to the entrepreneur may not be to others), Timely. These objectives will then help the planning process for implementation of the entrepreneurial activities.

It is also important to realize that objectives are dynamic and can change with the circumstances. The entrepreneurial individual should not allow themselves to be afflicted with tunnel vision and see things only in a narrow way; there may well be lateral opportunities to be grasped.

8. COMMUNICATE THE VISION

Whatever the vision of the entrepreneurial individual, it and its associated objectives need to be communicated to all those who will be involved with bringing it to fruition.

Others may not be as fired with enthusiasm as the generator of the ideas and for them the vision will need to be put forward clearly and concisely. There may well be those who see flaws in proposals – flaws that because of their zeal have not been noticed by the entrepreneur. These people should be listened to and cognizance given to their opinions. They may be right!

Writing the vision down in clear terms can provide a useful focus for people. It needs to become a shared vision if everybody is going to pull together.

9. ENSURE SUPPORT

The entrepreneur needs support both professionally and domestically. The continuing support of financiers, partners, suppliers, staff, and customers is obviously vital to the success of any venture. The earlier these people are taken into the entrepreneur's confidence (without letting out too many trade and proprietary secrets) the sooner they can "buy-in" to the project and feel a part of it.

The same is true for family. The individual needs to ensure that time is kept for family relationships. It can be difficult balancing the hard work and long hours that entrepreneurial activities require with a commitment to one's family, but it must be done.

If failure occurs, the support of colleagues and especially of family will be vital in the process of recovering and starting again. All entrepreneurs are going to experience failure at some point in their career and those who have speak loudly of the crucial role of their parents, partners, siblings, and wider family.

10. BUILD UP A NETWORK

Entrepreneurs rarely conduct just one project during their lives. As they move from activity to activity their network of contacts becomes more and more important to their success.

The entrepreneurial individual rarely lets an opportunity to network pass. Their Filofaxes and personal organizer memories are full of addresses and contacts. They are only too aware of the part other people play in their success.

The entrepreneurial individual needs to make networking a pro-activity thing. It is not just a question of meeting somebody but of retaining contact, indeed that is just as important as the first meeting. Remember nobody likes to feel that they are just being used and that the entrepreneur is interested in them only for what they can do for him or her. The successful entrepreneur will think carefully about what the other person will gain from the network.

KEY LEARNING POINTS

» Entrepreneurial individuals make things happen, they do not rely on luck.

» The entrepreneurial individual analyzes both the external environment and his or her strengths and weaknesses in order to maximize opportunities and guard against threats.

» No one, however entrepreneurial, can do everything on their own – they need the resources of other people.

» Entrepreneurs develop unique selling points to differentiate themselves and their activities from their competitors.

» Failure will happen – it is something to learn from, not to be afraid of.

Frequently Asked Questions (FAQs)

Q1: Can every individual be entrepreneurial?

A: In an ideal world, yes. The fact that you are reading this material suggests that you are already interested in the subject and this is the first step. However, entrepreneurism requires hard work, a tolerance of risk, and the development of certain skills and attributes. If you follow the ideas in this material, even if you do not become an entrepreneur as such, you will begin to carry out tasks in a more entrepreneurial way and you will be analyzing the environment in a constructive manner that can be transformed into pro-activity. It is worth contemplating that a world where everybody is a full-blown entrepreneur would have few who were happy carrying out routine tasks. However, a world where everybody is more entrepreneurial might well be a much more pleasant and exciting world.

There is more information about the requirements for entrepreneurism in Chapters 2, 3, 6, and 7.

Q2: What attributes must an entrepreneurial individual develop?

A: The entrepreneurial individual needs to develop the following attributes, all of which we possess to some extent:

» vision
» commitment
» self-belief
» discipline
» risk-taking
» concern for the customer
» creativity.

You can read about these attributes in more detail in Chapter 6.

Q3: What skills does an entrepreneurial individual need to acquire?

A: The entrepreneurial individual should ensure that they have acquired the following skills:

» analysis
» networking
» building relationships
» negotiation
» selling
» finance.

There is more detail on these skills in Chapter 6.

Q4: Surely failure is not something to countenance?

A: One should never aim to fail but failure is nevertheless bound to happen to entrepreneurs as they move into the unknown. Failure provides an opportunity to learn. One should never risk the whole enterprise but only undertake those activities where failure does not jeopardize organizational survival.

There is more about failure in Chapters 6 and 10.

Q5: I never take risks; can I still be an entrepreneur?

A: We all take risks every time we rise from our beds. However, if you really cannot stand risk-taking, then you should think very carefully about entrepreneurial activities. However, risk does provide a "buzz" and so it may be worth taking some small business risks and first see what happens and secondly see how you feel afterwards. Remember entrepreneurs only take calculated risks after careful consideration and analysis; anything else is foolhardy.

You can read more about risk-taking in Chapters 1, 6 and 7.

Q6: Is entrepreneurism about wealth?

A: No, entrepreneurs often become wealthy but this does not stop their activities. Entrepreneurship is about making progress, taking calculated risks, and doing things differently – it allows individuals to fulfill potential. Entrepreneurship may be hard work but it should also be fun!

For more information see Chapters 1, 2, 6 and 7.

Q7: Why are vision and objectives important to the entrepreneurial individual?

A: Vision provides an idea of the end point, although for most entrepreneurial individuals the end of one project signals the start of another. Objectives are the smaller steps to achieving the vision.

There are more details about vision and objectives in Chapters 2 and 6.

Q8: Does modern entrepreneurship have to involve computers and the Internet?

A: Many recent entrepreneurs have been involved in information technology, as that is the current area of greatest development. The UK inventor and entrepreneur James Dyson has made his name with vacuum cleaners and washing machines, Ken Bogas is a cook. The Internet is a useful tool for all entrepreneurs as it provides access to information and markets.

This is covered in more detail in Chapter 4.

Q9: What role do family, friends and colleagues have in supporting the entrepreneurial individual?

A: A considerable role. We all need somebody to share success and support us when things are not going well. Professional support may well include finance, etc., and domestic support may be emotional, an area of life often forgotten but of critical importance.

There is more about this subject both in terms of professional and domestic support in Chapter 6.

Q10: Where are resources available to assist in understanding the entrepreneurial individual?

A: A list of books, journals, and Web addresses will be found in Chapter 9.

Index

Printed and bound in the UK by
CPI Antony Rowe, Eastbourne

Printed and bound by CPI Group (UK) Ltd, Croydon, CR0 4YY

13/04/2025

14656561-0004